Praise for *Disarming High-Conflict Personalities*

"Jeff Riggenbach has created helpful, practical information for anyone to use who is looking for ways to better connect with other people. We all have difficult people in our lives. It only takes one person to change an environment and that one person can be you! It is a skill set that can be practiced and enjoyed. Learn how to become the change agent in your relationships and watch what happens in your daily life! Thank you, Jeff, for this helpful information. Great job!"

- Dr. Robert A. Rohm
President, Personality Insights, and
Co-Founder of discoveryreport.com

I so much enjoyed Dr Riggenbach's book on dealing with high conflict people. This is such a wise and practical book that sadly all of us need at times. Highly readable, highly relevant and exceptionally useful for the sharp elbows that we often confront in real life. Each chapter gives you specific concrete strategies and ways of defusing potential useless conflict. This is a no-nonsense guide to the real world. I know I will be recommending this book to my clients and... to myself!

- Robert L. Leahy, Ph.D.
Author, The Worry Cure Director,
American Institute of Cognitive Therapy

Dr. Jeff Riggenbach offers his readers a comprehensive and coherent peek into the science of human interaction in his thoughtfully written new book, "Disarming High Conflict Personalities…" This book is a must-read for all, chock full of clearly illustrated examples and creative strategies for dealing with some of the most challenging personality types we are all likely to confront in our lives, be it in our primary and family relationships, work affiliates, friendships, or casual day-to-day encounters.

~ Wendy Behary, Author/Expert
Disarming the Narcissist, 3rd Edition/2021

There is no such thing as a "bad" personality style. However, any style operating out of control can create difficulties in the workplace, school, or the church. Dr. Riggenbach's goal in this book was to avoid the clinical jargon and write a guide that is effective to help the everyday leader (you) learn to recognize these traits and then respond appropriately. This book is a must read for all leaders who need practical insights and tips for effectively dealing with high conflict personalities on the team in a way that benefits everyone.

~ Chris Rollins
President, Rollins Performance Group

DISARMING HIGH-CONFLICT PERSONALITIES:

Dealing with the Eight Most Difficult People in Your Life Before They Burn You Out

JEFF RIGGENBACH, PHD

Library of Congress Control Number: 2022900062

ISBN: 978-1-64746-989-4 (Paperback)
ISBN: 978-1-64746-990-0 (Hardback)
ISBN: 978-1-64746-991-7 (Ebook)

Cover design: Matthew Skar (matthew@theinchouse.com)
Additional design and publishing assistance: Dara Rogers (dara@darasdesign.com)
General copy editor: Tina Morlock (tinamorlock@gmail.com)
Behavioral health copy editor: Shannan Garbani (shanmarie23@gmail.com)

Author's Note

This book and accompanying coaching/consulting program are intended to give you tips, tools, and tidbits to help you deal with the difficult people in your life. While the eight "types" do represent specific personality styles with common predictable attitudes, behaviors, and responses, it should be noted that any model that puts people in categories is based on generalizations, and almost nobody fits perfectly into any one box. So recognize that there are exceptions. These suggestions and strategies for dealing with difficult personalities may not apply in all situations. You are advised to seek professional coaching, consultation, or counseling for direction with your specific case if expert advice is needed. The author and publisher are not responsible for any decisions or actions you take as a result of reading this book.

Also note that my assignment of names to these eight "difficult personalities" can be a fun and helpful way for you to remember and recognize types of people you may encounter so that you will know which types of strategies might be most helpful in dealing with them. However, actually using these names when talking to high-conflict individuals themselves will be hurtful to them and counterproductive for your goals. Use these *only* as a way of enhancing your understanding so that you may relate more effectively with the people in your life. I would submit that anyone who chooses to utilize these or other labels as weapons in relationships has some "difficult" in them as well!

Finally, while all case studies and examples are based on real-life situations, specific names, quotes, and details of clients and their situations are often altered to preserve anonymity and to best demonstrate the principles of the book.

Now read on to equip yourselves, and happy learning!

Best,
Jeff

Contents

Preface

Several people have asked me why I wrote this book. The answer is because it needed to be written. There are tens of thousands of personal development books in the marketplace. There are thousands of DISC trainers and many related publications and manuals. There is a plethora of clinical texts written by psychologists or other behavioral health professionals and even a few for the general public. But few if any exist for the general public that are clinically informed but also speak the language of the everyday person in leadership in workplace, educational, and faith-based settings.

First of all, my background of twenty years in the clinical world of psychology with specializations in cognitive behavioral therapy and treatment of personality disorders uniquely qualify me far beyond most organizational trainers, "gurus" or other personal development "experts." Second, after just having my second kidney transplant, my immune system was not ready to reenter clinical settings, especially in an era of COVID-19. So this is a season of my life in which I am spending a lot of time by myself. So, I figured, no better time, right?

As my sphere of influence expanded, not only through my international speaking and training, but also through my association with the John Maxwell Team, I ran into many folks from different walks of life who wondered why people in their lives behaved in specific ways. As I interacted with more people in nonclinical settings, I realized that people with some of the same distorted thinking and even personality disordered traits that my clients had were everywhere! Many people didn't have these problems to the same degree, but I noticed their problems were similar. They were just showing up in smaller ways and different settings. As I inched my way into the leadership development world, I made an additional observation: Organizations could have "personality disorders" as well! They spoke a whole different language. These organizations didn't call them "*symptoms*" or "*maladaptive behavioral patterns*." Instead, they used terms like "*culture problem*," "*employee satisfaction*," and "*workplace morale*." Neither did they use our clinical language of "*functional impairment*," but they spoke of things like "*hostile work environment complaints*," "*employee retention*," and the "*bottom line*." Regardless of the lingo used, these all refer to the same thing: negative outcomes resulting from an inability to deal effectively with people.

As my eyes opened a bit wider, I realized these difficult people aren't only at work. I noticed they could also be school administrators, teachers, and students. Clergy, church staff, and parishioners can also be categorized as difficult. I heard it described by civic leaders, government officials, and leaders in the nonprofit sector. And most of all, these people show up in our personal lives. They are our neighbors, our daughter's boyfriend, and sometimes they are even in our families!

Everybody thinks their situation is different. So many people told me things like "You could never understand—it's complicated."

I learned to say—and even with a smile—"Try me."

Because regardless of the details that came out of the person's mouth, they always told a story I knew well. It was like a recurring dream I experienced night after night. Only this time I knew how it ended. It felt like being stuck in a cycle from the movie *Groundhog Day*. Story after story after story. The manifestations may have looked a little different than what I was used to seeing in the clinical setting—but the issue always stayed the same: people having trouble dealing with very specific types of people.

Here's the good news: There are themes in their behaviors and your reactions to these challenging individuals. And that human behavior is more of a science than an art. So even if you think your situation is unique or the difficult person in your life is "impossible," I promise you there is a way out.

So, because I have seen hundreds if not thousands of these situations over the past twenty years, know what to look for, and helped many people overcome these relational obstacles, in the pages that follow, I will guide you through what you need to understand so you can speak in a manner that others will always hear you.

My best to you as you seek to disarm the difficult people in your life.

Jeff

INTRODUCTION

Difficult People Are Everywhere!

A couple of years ago, I was flying back from a conference I spoke at in Canada and we had an extended delay at Atlanta Airport. As I kicked back in the gate area chitchatting with the lady sitting next to me, we observed the reactions of fellow passengers on the flight as everybody experienced an increased level of frustration the longer they delayed the flight. While we watched, we noticed four consecutive individuals walk up to the counter and say essentially the same thing to the gate agent. But they said very different things.

The first guy brashly stomped up to the podium and in a harsh and borderline threatening tone of voice said, "I cannot believe this flight is delayed again! I have an important meeting to get to—I demand to be on the next flight out of this airport!" Next, a lady spun dramatically up to the podium and, in a delicate and almost attention-seeking manner said, "I cannot believe another flight is delayed! When I flew out on this very trip, and we were also delayed they pulled out that little beanbag toss game. Do you guys have one of those at this terminal? Maybe someone could order pizza! We could have a party!"

The third person to approach the podium was a lady who did so in a very timid manner. Her nonverbal's screamed apology before she even actually opened her mouth. She said, "I almost hate to even ask. I know this is a stressful situation. But, maybe, if it isn't too much trouble, I am trying to get home and visit my grandmother in the hospital. Is there any way you could possibly, see if there are any other flights out tonight?" The fourth was a gentleman who sauntered up to the podium in a very rigid manner wearing a three-piece suit and carrying a pocket protector. (I can't make this stuff up). He stated, "This flight has been delayed one hour and thirty-seven minutes to date. My flight connects in Minneapolis at six thirty-two. Based on previous experience in that airport it takes me nineteen minutes to get from terminal C, which from my app I see is where we are scheduled to land, to terminal A where my connecting flight is scheduled to depart from—is there any more efficient way for you to get me where I need to go?"

As we sat there chuckling, the lady next to me said, "Oh, people are so different."

And they are.

But they are also the same.

That's why this is funny. As I described this scene, some of you were undoubtedly saying, "Oh my gosh, that is my spouse." Others of you saw one of your coworkers. Maybe you noticed traits of your children or your parents or maybe even yourself!

If you know the DISC model of personality, you might say, "Hey, one of those was a *D*, one was an *I*, one was an *S* and the last one was a *C!*"

If you understand clinical language, you might say, "Hey, one of those was narcissistic, one was histrionic, one was dependent, and one was obsessive-compulsive!"

At the end of this book, you will know a little of both.

These observations are backed by science. There are recognizable patterns of human behavior. Once you understand how these patterns work, you will have the most powerful tool you need for dealing with all people—particularly the difficult people in your life.

Although there are thousands of "conflict management" books out there, since my background involves twenty years in the clinical world of psychology overseeing treatment of some of the most difficult people in the world, this book will provide a depth 99 percent of speakers and authors in this area cannot. However, even though we clinical people do have psychobabble terms for "jerk," "nerd," "needy chick," and a variety of others, this book will use everyday language we all know to describe the people who make life a little more complicated than it needs to be. And, most importantly, it will show you how to handle them in a manner that will no longer allow them to drive you nuts!

You know them. We all have them in our lives.

- ♣ The boss who has ascended to a position of authority due to connections but has more testosterone than talent
- ♣ The lunatic uncle who thinks you care about his political and religious opinions
- ♣ The crazy ex who needs a copy of Webster's to understand the meaning of the word "No"

- ♣ The incompetent coworker who always wants to take credit for your ideas
- ♣ The student who is more interested in being the class clown than learning
- ♣ The member of your congregation who has nothing better to do in life than stir up dissension and gossip among others
- ♣ The smother mother who won't stay out of your business

High-conflict (HC) people ruin morale in work groups, create tension in educational settings, promote divisiveness in church congregations, and disrupt family dynamics, robbing people of their joy.

Difficult people are why good employees leave companies.

Companies create their cultures by the people they choose to hire, the values they choose to operate by, and the priorities they choose to emphasize.

Sometimes companies look for the wrong things (or at least emphasize them). For instance, a person who has a vision for the future and a charismatic presence in the room may be brought on by senior management without recognition of the fact that he/she also has low empathy and does not value the opinions of others. The decision-maker(s) overseeing the move were so focused on the candidate's ability to articulate a vision for the company with charm that they simply missed the potential downside to his personality.

Some school administrators put too much focus on hiring someone with the organizational skills to prepare and present a quality lesson and completely miss that the teacher lacks the frustration tolerance to deal with challenging behaviors in the classroom or demonstrate actual concern for the students.

Some organizations hire difficult people unintentionally. While no decision-maker intends to hire high-maintenance employees, many simply fail to do their due diligence. CEOs appoint their buddies to leadership posts who are not qualified to run that particular area. Small business owners don't have vast resources at their disposal, and the president often thinks "I am a good judge of character" and assumes that will be enough. And sometimes it is. However, while many leaders could sniff out someone who might be transporting dead bodies in their trunk, few can pick up on subtle nuances in candidates that frequently make all the difference in organizational culture and performance. Qualities such as poor initiative, attention-seeking, passive-aggressiveness, and other many other traits are not as easily detected and can poison the work environment from day one.

Everyone has heard the expression "one bad apple spoils the barrel." Likewise, it only takes one difficult person in the workplace to kill morale, plummet employee retention, sink productivity, and ultimately inadvertently sabotage organizational goals.

Difficult students drive teachers to find a different profession. Or, worse, they continue to teach but get bitter and burned out.

As our society continues to deteriorate, the breakdown of the family becomes more and more apparent in schools. Teachers find themselves in "parental" roles. Lack of supervision, nurturing, and discipline at home contribute to increased emotional and behavioral problems at school. Teachers are now not only being asked to be teachers, but also parents, psychologists, dietitians, law enforcement, and general caregivers.

Divisive and confrontational troublemakers make board meetings unproductive, church congregations unhealthy, and nonprofit organizations dysfunctional. Unhealthy personal relationships become the norm as a result.

Relationships have become more shallow, chaotic, and punitive. People have become more self-centered. Families concern themselves with how things look over how things are. Likewise, many companies are more concerned with public image and perception than the welfare of their employees. "Presenting well" trumps authenticity and genuineness. Getting ahead is valued over getting it right.

Good employees want to quit. Teachers only want to make it through the day. Clergy feel helpless in the face of the chaos.

You get the picture. Difficult people exist everywhere in life. And we don't get a choice about *whether* or not we interact with them. Our only choice is *how* we interact with them. Occasionally I run into people who say, *"Well I just don't deal with difficult people—that's how I deal with them."* If this is what you think, I hate to break it to you, but that probably means YOU ARE SOMEBODY'S DIFFICULT PERSON!

Hope is not a strategy

Here's the good news: We get to choose how we react to others. The reality is that we have ZERO percent control over what other people do. And, we have 100 percent control over how we respond to what other people do. And contrary to popular belief, there are effective ways to respond to these people. Just because someone invites us to an argument doesn't mean we have to accept the invitation. But we must learn the strategies for not taking their bait. And then we need to learn how to transition from defense to offense.

There is a strategy involved. In 2015, the Oklahoma City Thunder fired their head coach Scott Brooks. Although his winning percentage bested many of his peers, he couldn't figure out how to win a championship with some of the most elite talent in the NBA. Up until the 2014 season, the Thunder had Kevin Durant, Russell Westbrook, and James Harden, three of the NBA's most prolific all-stars and sure-fire future hall of famers. Yet, despite all that talent, Brooks developed a reputation of not understanding how to use it effectively. The simple act of drawing up out of bounds play seemed an insurmountable task. A leading ESPN basketball analyst put it this way:

"Be great," is not a strategy. It was as though Brooks was only sending his team out on the court and saying "be great" but could not devise a game plan to use the greatness he had on his roster in a way that could maximize their potential.

"Talent acquisition" is not enough in business. Likewise, hoping your students will behave on a given day accomplishes little. How many times have you heard a well-meaning family member say a version of "just hang in there—things will get better—don't give up."

Have you wanted to ask, *"How do you know?"*

Just as "be great" is not a strategy, neither is hope a strategy. As Henry Ford is often credited with saying, "If you keep doing what you've always done, you'll always get what you always got." We must be strategic about how we approach situations. Handling people is no different. Some factors are out of our hands. We have no control over natural disasters, the traffic on the way to work, or other people's behavior. But we do influence more than most of us realize. And if we, or others, contribute to the problem in ways we don't realize, "hoping" things will get better is futile if not counterproductive. But if we learn to be aware of our role in situations and be more intentional about how we deal with them, we really can learn to influence difficult people to stop doing the things we don't want them to do and start doing the things we do want them to do.

I've designed the following chapters to help you understand what makes these high-conflict people tick. You will learn red flags for spotting them sooner, how to read them, how to speak their language so you can talk to them in a way they will hear you, and ultimately how to respond in ways that make your life easier.

There is a science to understanding and handling high-conflict personalities. And make no mistake, dealing with the difficult people life throws at us is never easy. It is hard interactional work. And we all get to decide if it's worth the effort. But as the world's number one leadership expert (if you don't believe me, just google it☺) John C. Maxwell says, "everything worth having is uphill." Learning to deal effectively with challenging people in life *is* often an uphill battle.

However, since we don't have a choice and this is a battle we will all have to fight, most people would rather learn how to fight a winning battle.

The following chapters will show you how, more often than not, to fight that winning battle.

You will learn the intricacies of how high-conflict people think, how they feel, and *why* they behave in the "difficult" ways—and, most importantly, how to respond when they do. As a result, you might even learn not to dread these people. As we become more skilled at dealing with the people who make life hard, believe it or not, we can come to see challenging people as opportunities for growth!

And, perhaps just as importantly, it will help you decide when it is time to cut bait and move on. Finally, it will aid you in taking charge of your personal life in a way you didn't know was possible, creating the life you want to live, surrounded by the people who make it worthwhile.

So sit back, relax and enjoy the ride.

1

The Secret to Understanding all People: A Model for Human Behavior

People don't often behave the way we think they should. As Greg Lester puts it, "Everyone behaves badly at times. And some people behave badly a great deal of the time."

However, since there are several different ways to "behave badly," nothing works all the time. That's why most personal development and self-help books are practically worthless. They teach things like "assertiveness" as if they are always a good thing. I am reminded of my client who once passionately told me, "I tried what you taught us this week about being assertive, but it completely backfired! That's the last time I try what you taught me—it blew up in my face!"

I said, "I'm sorry it didn't work for you this time. Do you want to tell me the story?"

She responded, "There's no story. I just tried standing up for myself like you taught us but that cop didn't appreciate it!"

As with every other communication skill, assertiveness is helpful in some contexts and unhelpful in others. So personal development books that advocate only one thing—such as "making your voice heard" or "taking massive action" only have value in situations where that is the best course of action for a person in that particular situation. They are actually *counterproductive* when used in contexts that call for a different interpersonal strategy. I have worked with clients who got expelled from their universities for "making their voice heard" when not happy with a teacher's enforcement of a policy. I worked with a pastor who "took massive action" without consulting a municipal governing body and got in a lot of trouble. A different client was urged by a previous life coach to "face his fear" of driving by hopping in his car and "just doing it" (before he had the skill level or confidence to do so.) The man had an accident, ended up spending a week in the hospital, and killed two other people in an oncoming car in the process. "Making your voice heard," "taking massive action," and "facing your fears" all sound like "good" things. They are all useful skills to have. However, they are only helpful when used strategically and selectively based on the people involved and the specifics of the situation.

What is "good" and what is "bad" usually if not always differs according to context. I encourage my clients to use the terms *helpful versus unhelpful*. A former client of mine learned his critical and discerning mind was beneficial to him at work in his role as a mechanic. It was his job to diagnose what was "wrong" with people's cars so he would know what to fix. His critical eye for finding what went "wrong" aided him to the point that he developed a reputation as the best diagnostician in the area. Patrons paid good money to get his eyes on their vehicles because they knew he could find and fix the malfunction quicker and better than any of his competition. However, that critical mind that always saw what was wrong in something did not serve him nearly as well in his failing marriage or tumultuous relationship with his two children. Just because a tool or trait "works" in one setting or situation, doesn't mean it will in others.

The opposite is also true. Many coaching and therapy clients need to hear that just because a tool doesn't work in certain settings doesn't mean it won't work in others.

Abraham Maslow famously amplified the proverb "If all you have is a hammer, everything you see looks like a nail."

Since we can't apply the same skill in every context, we must not only learn the necessary skills so we have them in our repertoire, but also learn the strategy of knowing which skills to use with what people and in which situations.

Being a tennis player, this made perfect sense to me the first time I heard it. Every day in high school and college tennis practice we would do drills. I learned the skills of how to hit a forehand and a backhand. I learned the form necessary to execute crisp volleys. I developed the ability to hit approach shots, drop shots, lobs, and overhead smashes. I understood the detailed mechanical differences between hitting a serve with topspin versus hitting a serve with slice.

But all these skills I learned would be useless if I didn't also know strategy—if I didn't use my skills in very intentional ways during actual matches. I could be the most *skilled* player in the tournament, but if I hit volleys from the baseline, drop shots when my opponent was at the net, and swung as hard as I could on every serve, I would inevitably lose every match.

I saw a meme on Facebook not long ago posted by a prominent personal development "guru" who does many corporate and public training events that said, "Normal is just a setting on the washing machine." In today's nonjudgmental world, it is trendy to put out normalizing messages such as this to facilitate acceptance of all behaviors. I attended a lecture by a cardiologist one time where he made the point that there are thousands of variances in the human heart. Yet physicians have ways of differentiating cardiac diseases from healthy heart functioning.

Similarly, there *is* such a thing as "normal" or "healthy" personality functioning. John Oldham defines healthy personality function as "the magnificent variety of non-pathological behaviors." People with "normal" or "healthy" personalities can do this. They can "turn on" and "turn off" parts of their personalities so to speak, to fit the situation at hand and use the skill that will be most effective in dealing with any person at any moment.

In contrast to my client described above, people with healthy personality function can put on their critical thinking hats in situations that it serves them to do so—and they can also take that hat off and be more compassionate, affirming, and positive in environments where those traits are called for. We might say they know to hit overhead smashes from the net, drop shots when their opponent is deep in the court out of position, and strategically use pace and placement to their advantage depending on the specific opponent and circumstances of the point.

People with high-conflict or otherwise difficult personalities lack the ability to turn their traits on and off according to context. They know only one "way to be."

And when that "way" does not fit their circumstances or interactions, they have a unique way of creating a crisis. And a chaos that not only disrupts their lives but often overflows uninvited into the lives of those around them.

So here is the secret. Contrary to what celebrities and new age gurus tell us, it is NOT *think it and we will manifest it*. The secret is understanding that there is power in *recognizing patterns of human behavior and using highly specialized skills in strategic ways for dealing differently with different people.*

Human beings behave the way they do based on their learned patterns of behavior—not the way we think they *should* behave. Once we (1) recognize the pattern of behavior in the person we are interacting with, and (2) accept that they will behave that way regardless of what we think, we can respond to them much more effectively.

Why?

Because when we no longer expect disloyal people to keep our confidence, self-centered people to look out for our best interest, or people without a spine to stand up for a principle, we don't get as internally worked up when they don't. And, when we know what to expect based on *their established patterns of behavior* rather than our preferences, we can then respond in calmer ways to employ purposeful interactional strategies for dealing with them in more beneficial ways. But we must recognize the patterns so we can know whether to choose the hammer or go back to the toolbox for a more appropriate tool.

Now you know the secret, let's get to work!

The work starts by learning how to identify patterns in people's behavior.

Many models exist for conceptualizing human behavior. There are also many theories, ways of thinking about it, and different personality tests as well. I have worked with most of them over the years, from more clinical models to the MMPI to Myers–Briggs, to other trendier but less scientifically proven approaches such as the enneagram. Having worked with assessments that run the gamut of scientific credibility, I actually surprised myself when I came to prefer the DISC. I do believe it is the most practical, effective way for working with everyday folks. Its "styles" are more consistent with established cognitive science of thinking and behavior than any of its "competitors" that claim to do similar things. Additionally, DISC offers the added benefit of not only facilitating awareness into our own personality style, but also giving us the ability to understand others quickly. These insights can help us communicate and connect with others in more meaningful and influential ways.

The DISC was developed in 1928 by Harvard psychologist William Marston. Some may find it interesting that he is not only the same man who pioneered the lie detector test, but that he was also the creator of *Wonder Woman,* whose weapon was the "lasso of truth." While the model may seem quite simple, as we walk through its foundational principles (this book does not delve into more advanced aspects of the tool such as graphs, style blends, etc.), know that it is based on his early research on statistical patterns of human behavior and I have found it to be surprisingly accurate.

The model starts by identifying if a person is primarily *outgoing* or primarily *reserved*. People identified as "outgoing" or having "high energy" or being more "fast-paced" would fall in the top half of the circle below depicting the model.

It then identifies if a person is primarily *task oriented* or *people oriented*. Although all of us typically have a mixture of these traits, here's a highly "scientific" way to tell:

Do you lie in bed at night thinking, "I sure did get a lot done today. I got this done—check ... and that done—check. It sure was a great day!"?

Or, do you lie in bed thinking, "It sure was great to see her today, and I had a great conversation with so-and-so, and I sure hope he is doing OK."

It doesn't mean that those who are primarily people oriented can't feel good because they accomplish things and it doesn't mean that task-oriented people don't take any satisfaction from relationships. But typically people are "fueled" primarily by one or the other. It may not come as a surprise to you that Personality Insights research has estimated that 90 percent of human conflict is between task-oriented people and people-oriented people.

Those who primarily identify with being task oriented would then fall on the left half of the circle, whereas persons more people oriented would be placed on the right.

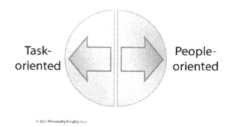

Even those of us who are not overly gifted in geometry might now recognize that we have four quadrants, two made up of outgoing and two of which consist of reserved. We also have overlapping quadrants, two of which consist of task oriented and two made up of people oriented. According to the DISC model then, the person identified as primarily *outgoing* AND *task oriented* would fall in the upper left-hand quadrant and be classified as a **D**. The person who identified as *outgoing* and *people oriented* would fall in the upper right quadrant and be classified as an **I**. Someone who identified as *reserved* and *people oriented* would be placed in the lower right quadrant and classified as an **S**. Finally, those identified as primarily reserved and task oriented would fall in the lower left quadrant and be categorized as a **C**.

You may be familiar with the terms "right brain" versus "left brain." Although the latest brain research has shown the brain is not nearly as dichotomous as we once believed, the term "right brain" has typically referred to people with *I* and *S* styles while the term "left brain" has often been applied to *D's* and *C's*. This basic model has been taught in many ways over the years. I originally learned these in high school as the "Lion," the "Otter," the "Golden Retriever," and the "Beaver." You may also be familiar with the terms choleric, sanguine, phlegmatic, and melancholy, just to name a few.

Research from the corporate world tells us that the average salesperson typically makes half of their sales to people who match their style. Those who learn more about the styles of others drastically increase their conversions. Since the goal of many people reading this book may not be sales, "conversions" may look quite different. What if you could learn how to get someone in your personal life, church, nonprofit, or the board you serve on to stop engaging in a certain problem behavior? What if you could gain new insights about your coworkers, boss, or employees that would enable you to be much more effective in the workplace? What if you could learn to manage classroom behaviors in ways you previously did not know were possible?

Although you only need a skeleton version of the model to understand the concepts in this book, DISC certainly offers solutions for dealing with people on the job, has implications for how teachers could seat their classrooms, and offers interpersonal effectiveness skills that will help you beyond this book's purpose.

Here is the overview of the four general DISC styles that will provide the foundation for the different types of difficult people we will discuss.

The Dominant type (D)

Prevalence: 10 percent of the population
Motto: "Do it now!"
Descriptive words: Dominant, doer, direct, determined
Ideal environment: One in which they have the freedom to make decisions and set their own pace
Strengths: Generates ideas, takes the initiative, works hard, gets things done, provides leadership
Weaknesses: Can lack patience, empathy, and hurt others' feelings
Triggered by: Slow paces, long drawn-out explanations, anything that impedes productivity.

D's have been called natural-born leaders. If you want to get something done, the *D* is your go-to guy (or gal). They are usually the most confident people in your group. *D's* are the most productive employees on your team. They are the leaders in your classroom. They drive the initiatives where you volunteer, organize ministry projects at your church, and lead the discussions at your meetings. They are full of energy. They are fiercely driven to "win," and are fueled by doing so. To the extent that you have some *D* in you, you might enjoy making those checklists—and the more boxes you check off your to-do list, the better you feel. As stated above, as you lie in bed at night and reflect on your "good" day, it typically consisted of a nice run of accomplishments in which you were able to "check" multiple boxes.

It is, however, important not to mistake the *D's* spontaneous impulses to take massive action as just a need to stay busy. We all know people who just have to stay busy. However, contrary to the "workaholic" or the "busybody," who is usually avoiding something in their life, the *D* is doing what they are doing for a different reason. Rather than running from something, they are genuinely fueled by the pursuit of accomplishment and the bottom line is as important as the top line. There is always a specific goal on their radar or a larger purpose that will breed feelings of accomplishment and mastery if met.

If you have a high amount of "*D*," you are probably one of the most productive people on your team, in your group, and in your classrooms. You lead projects. You finish assignments and tests before anyone in your class. And after doing so, you don't lose energy—you are ready to move on to the next obstacle to conquer!

Also of note is that the *D* is on the opposite end of the spectrum from the *C* in terms of evaluating risk. *D's* tend to underestimate risk, if they even consider it at all. *C's*, on the other hand, overestimate risk. That's one of the reasons it takes them so long to get things done. Remember the *D's* motto. Their primary motive is to "do it now!" Quality of performance and human relationships are secondary in their mindset.

In addition to the strengths, every style has weaknesses. *D's* burning desires to accomplish, and "win" can come at the expense of other people. They often lack patience, as well as the ability to put themselves in others' shoes. Their direct and sometimes brash communication style can run people over and hurt feelings. If you have a fair amount of *D* in you, your thought process may be something like "well, we hurt a few people's feelings along the way, but we got the job done and we met our deadline. That's the most important thing. Those sensitive people sometimes have to be collateral damage."

Confidence can actually become a detriment if unchecked. Epictetus was talking about the extreme *D* when he said, "It is impossible to begin to learn that which one thinks one already knows."

When dealing with the **D**, it is important to get to the point quickly. Remember they are performance oriented and extremely competitive. Keep in mind that they like to win as quickly as possible so they can move on to their next win. Long, rambling conversations are unnecessary obstacles in the way of their next win and becoming an impediment to their victory is a good way to get on their bad side.

They desire to "get right to it" and they want you to do the same.

Remember they are "left brained" individuals. Approach them with logic, use facts, and be credible. Utilizing these ingredients will avoid triggering the **D** and you will be less likely to provoke a harsh reply. Most importantly, focus on results. Identify the result most important to the **D** and make that a focal point of your communication with them.

The Influencing type (I)

Prevalence: 25 percent of the population
Motto: "Do it fun!"
Descriptive words: Inspiring, influential, impulsive, intuitive, imaginative
Ideal environment: Positive, jovial environment where others handle the details
Strengths: Energetic, fun, spontaneous, humorous
Weaknesses: Can have difficulty following through with tasks, lose focus or be shallow
Triggered by: Boredom, feeling ignored.

I's are the life of the party. They love to entertain, and they thrive on making things fun. Occasionally, they might even act a little dramatic. They are emotional and spontaneous. They are the epitome of the "right brained" individual who is innovative, creative and "touchy-feely." Their mindset is often "we didn't meet that deadline today, but we sure had a blast working on it!"

I's are usually the type of person you like to be around. They are often the reason others want to go to work. They can have a way of making work seem like it is not even work! They are class clowns who have an innate ability to make everyone else laugh and help loosen other students up before an important exam. Their passion draws people in and they have a way of bringing out the fun side in others. Their love for life is infectious. *I's* can even make meetings fun again!

In terms of weaknesses, the reality is that life isn't always fun. Some situations in life call for seriousness, focus, and task completion. The *I's* fun can come at the expense of getting the important things done or dealing with the necessities of life. Many of you could probably attest to some of the problems that can arise when a team member at work always has to be the center of attention. Perhaps some of you have started to date someone who was absolutely one of the most fun people you have been around—but, when you tried to get them to go a little deeper or have a meaningful discussion they were always deflecting or making some superficial joke. Finally *I's* can fall victim to a version of *shiny object syndrome.* Any of you who have a little *I* in you can testify to having difficulty reading an entire book—not because you were incapable of it, but because before you got halfway through it you had already found three others you wanted to start!

When dealing with *I's*, it is important to keep things friendly and fun. Knowing they can get bored or distracted easily, do what you can to make the environment friendly and keep them engaged. Give them opportunities to interact in the classroom and group projects when possible at work.

Validate them often and keep them moving. At church, find a coffee area, a place for socializing, or even time to stand and greet those around you. These are ideal ways to invigorate the *I before, during, or after the service.* When *I's* get bored, they often disengage from work, you will lose them in the classroom, and they might even resign and move on to something else.

The Social type (S)

Prevalence: 35 percent of the population
Motto: "Do it together!"
Descriptive words: Social, stable, sincere
Ideal environment: Supportive, stable environment with regular communication
Strengths: Supportive, dependable, trustworthy
Weaknesses: Can lack assertiveness, be overly talkative or have poor boundaries
Triggered by: Rejection, perception of not being liked, being asked for help

S's are all about relationships. Since they are "people-people," humans and their feelings are more important than tasks. By a long way. Similar to the *I*, they may have many friends, but to the *S*, the *quality* of the relationship is more important than the *quantity* of relationships or the attention they receive. They are the most dependable, trustworthy, and loyal friends we could ask for, and they will be there with you through thick and thin. If you have some *S* in your personality, you may recognize yourself lying in bed at night thinking about the conversations you had that day or the relationships you have in your life. These thoughts could focus on either worrying about the well-being or feelings of someone you care about or feeling satisfied with uplifting or supportive interactions you had that day. Your mindset is "wow, we got that project done on time, but it really bothers me that Amy got her feelings hurt."

Since *S's* are the most trustworthy people you could hope to have in your life, they usually make faithful partners, supportive mentors, and fiercely loyal friends. They encourage like no other and are the most supportive people on the planet. They go the extra mile for others and will often sacrifice themselves to further the best interest of others. *S's* make the most dependable and reliable employees, the most nurturing clergy or caretakers, and the most stable and supportive parents.

On the downside, *S's* are far more prone to get their feelings hurt than the other styles. They frequently take comments personally that were not intended to be. Their need to be liked by others can be debilitating if not kept in check. Since relationships are the most important thing to the *S*, they can get triggered when there is tension in one. This heightened sensitivity to the words of others can make them more vulnerable to mood swings when they experience friction in their personal life. They tend to obsess over interpersonal concerns to the point that it impacts their ability to accomplish tasks at work or assignments in school until the relationship is restored. Organization is usually not a strength, and their inability to tell others no can get them derailed easily. While the *I* can get distracted in an "ADD type of way" and have difficulty with task completion, *S's* inability to tell others no can lead to a similar result. These distractions occur not because they forgot what they were supposed to accomplish or even when the deadline was—but rather due to prioritizing someone else's request or emotional need over the task they were required to complete. In more extreme forms this self-sacrificing can contribute to codependent behaviors, enabling, or general difficulty meeting the responsibilities of everyday life.

Never underestimate the importance of relationships and feelings when dealing with the *S*. They are not difficult people to get along with until you forget this. Do what you can to make them feel safe and genuinely valued. Simple acknowledgment and/or validation of feelings can go a long way toward connecting with an *S*. Managers who learn to validate and show appreciation for these employees are often amazed at the skyrocket they see in work performance once they learn to do so. Students with *S* personality styles are much more likely to respond to teachers who have a strong nurturing quality than those who appear more rigid and rules oriented. Do what you can to reassure the *S* and be cognizant of their feelings and the emotions of those around them, and you will do fine with the **S**. You might even have a friend for life.

The Cautious type (C)

Prevalence: 30 percent of the population
Motto: "Do it right!"
Descriptive words: Cautious, calculating, competent, correctness, careful
Ideal environment: Given expectations and the freedom to work out the details
Strengths: Accurate, thorough, precise, produce the highest quality work
Weaknesses: Have difficulty meeting deadlines, lacks efficiency, emotionally cold, or critical
Triggered by: Micromanaging, vagueness, being Rushed

C's are cautious and careful. They represent the stereotypical "left brain" person. They are the most analytical ones among us. *C's* are often highly intelligent. They are logical, rational thinkers. People with this style make great problem-solvers are usually the reason projects and tasks get done well.

As alluded to earlier, *C's* fall on the opposite end of the spectrum from the *D* in terms of evaluating risk. While *D's* underestimate risk (or don't consider it at all to begin with), *C's* overestimate it. That is one of the reasons it can take them excessive amounts of time to accomplish tasks.

There are obvious benefits to this analyzing personality type. As mentioned above, their attention to detail ensures they complete tasks in a high-quality manner. There are many areas where we need people who prioritize their attention to detail over the speed of task completion, getting noticed, or making sure someone feels good in the process. We want airline mechanics, surgeons and people who run quality control to have these traits. These strengths often lead them to succeed in math, science, computing, and other technology-related fields. *C's* help partners think through various aspects of projects before jumping right in and acting in a counterproductive way. Careful consideration and critical thinking can contribute to academic success. In today's world, churches and nonprofits even need audiovisual, sound, and tech support to survive in ways not needed in years past.

Possessing such a deliberate style has drawbacks as well. For example, *C's* have trouble meeting deadlines. If you notice some of this trait in you, you likely may not be the most efficient person in your department, you could have some trouble delegating (because nobody else will do it the "right" way), and you might get annoyed at people trying to "rush" you. Others in your life may even verbalize being bothered by your difficulty expressing emotions or a tendency to be overly critical at times.

Employees with high *C* traits often slow their teams down, and students with significant *C* traits may have trouble completing tests in the required amount of time. The "can't see the forest for the trees" expression was developed because of *C's*, whose hyper focus can lead them to miss the big picture.

When interacting with *C's*, then, it is vital to remember the importance of *details* and *accuracy*. Remember that the words "good enough" are curse words to this style. Give specifics. Use statistics when possible. Cite facts. Validate their attention to detail where it is helpful, acknowledge the lack of quality work in a given area, and challenge them to become part of the solution rather than staying fixated on the problem.

So, there is your snapshot of the DISC. It is important to remember we are all a unique blend of these four general types. Although it is outside the scope of this book to do so, we could provide a more in-depth exploration of forty-one (41) different plotting points and explore the differences in personality nuances for each. My live organizational training sessions, live and virtual workshops and coaching sessions do just that. However, for our purposes, this basic look at the fundamentals will provide the foundation you will need to understand the specific types of high-conflict personalities this book will equip you to deal with.

2

What Makes People Difficult?

W e throw terms like "difficult person" around pretty haphazardly in today's society. Unfortunately, oftentimes, this is simply code for "I don't like him." Seemingly millions of people these days claim to be the victims of "narcissists." A quick informal search yielded over three hundred Facebook groups or pages devoted to dealing with narcissists in some form or fashion! Yet according to the American Psychological Association, just over 1 percent of the population meets the criteria for a narcissistic disorder! Of course, this does not negate the fact that many people worldwide have been and continue to be on the receiving end of some pretty terrible behavior perpetuated by people with narcissistic traits. But it suggests that there aren't enough narcissists in the world to account for the number of people claiming to be victims of their abuse.

The point? It is always easier to call somebody else a name than take responsibility for one's own role in a failed relationship or intense interaction.

Eleanor Roosevelt is often credited for saying a version of "nobody can offend me without my consent." Unfortunately, our hypersensitive, politically correct world has enabled distorted and victim-based thinking by placing no responsibility on the people who are constantly offended and all the blame on the "insensitive" people who make comments with no malicious intent.

This book guards against feeding into a victim mentality and strives to empower you to understand their behavior better. To do so, it is important to establish some criteria for what makes people "difficult."

Difficult people are more than just those who don't do the things we want them to and do the things we don't want them to. They aren't just people we don't like. And if they are not difficult to everyone and are only "difficult" to you, the problem may be you!

Though it is important to avoid name-calling and take responsibility for our actions, the reality is that there are many people out there that just make life more difficult than it needs to be. And they are the reason you are reading this book. So let's examine who these people might be and what makes them that way.

Contrasting styles

In cognitive therapy circles, we have the psychobabble terms *performance-oriented schemas* versus *sociotropic schemas*. In DISC language, this basically translates to *task-oriented* people versus *people-oriented* people. Personality Insights research on personality has shown that 90 percent of conflict occurs between task-oriented people and people-oriented people. In terms of the specific styles, *D's* and *C's* often view *S's* and *I's* as the most difficult and vice versa.

Consider the following scenarios:

♣ If your style is a *D*, how annoying is it to you when you want to jump right into a group project and a member of your team who is an *S* wants to do an icebreaker to get to know each other first?

♣ If you are an educator whose style is a *D* and you want your class to win the school-wide competition, how do you feel when your three *I* students clowning around is holding your class back?

♣ If your style is a *C* and you are going on your first business trip with a group of people with whom you have never traveled before—and you think you have your three-day itinerary planned out, but your supervisor, who is a high *I*, makes spontaneous decisions that require your participation all three evenings at social outings, how do you feel about him?

♣ If you are a pastor of a large church whose style is an *I* and you are excited to get in front of your congregation to unveil the latest service project, how much do you have to tame your tongue when the *C* on your committee wants to know *all* of the details related to how every penny involved will be allocated before you go public?

♣ If your style is an *S* and you are serving as the lead on the hospitality team for your convention, how bothered are you by the *D* on your committee who views each item as a "checkbox" to be accomplished in preparation for the event rather than opportunities to serve people and make them feel welcome?

Countless examples and scenarios exist for contrasting styles can cause friction. Even without "out of control" personalities involved, differences in style can cause us to view someone else as "difficult." Sometimes we just perceive them as difficult because their priorities are different than ours. It is important that we not assume that "because he was so driven and not concerned enough about her feelings, he is a bad person," or "because she just wanted to gab so much and slowed down our progress, she is a less valuable member of the team."

While the majority of the conflict comes from task-oriented thinking "butting heads" with people-oriented thinking, problems can also arise from the clashing of the other quadrants. For example, consider the following scenarios in which more reserved people perceive more outgoing people as difficult and vice versa.

- ♣ You are an attorney whose style is a *D*, and you are trying to prep a witness with strong *C* traits. You try to get them to answer only the questions you ask, but they feel compelled to give unnecessary details that make them vulnerable to additional attacks.

- ♣ As an *S*, you are completely embarrassed when your boss, whose style is an *I*, catches you off guard and calls you up in front of the entire crowd at the national convention to give you recognition.

- ♣ Your student, who is a high *C*, has difficulty completing assignments by your assigned deadlines. When testing comes around, she has the highest percentage correct of all the students but could not finish her work in time. As a *D*, you don't understand what takes her so long.

- ♣ Your newlywed spouse, who has more *I* in her than you realized before you married, has secretly put together a spur-of-the-moment weekend getaway. Naturally, as a high *C*, you want to know how long it will take to get there, what time she made the dinner reservations for, and how she possibly expects you to pack on a moment's notice.

♣ You are a *C* attending a new church. You feel as comfortable as you can in a new environment until, during the announcements, the pastor, whose style is an *I*, starts hamming it up on stage and asks everyone else to stand up and hug the person on either side of them!

As you can see, differing personality styles can create conflict in several ways. If you examine the circle closely, you can see that on one hand, every style has at least one thing in common with two of the other three general styles. And every letter has *one* polar opposite they have nothing in coming with.

For instance, the *D* shares the task-oriented trait with the *C* and the outgoing trait with the *I*, but has nothing in common with the *S*.

The *I* shares the outgoing trait with the *D* and the people-oriented trait with the *S*, but has nothing in common with the *C*.

The *S* shares the people-oriented trait with the *I* and the reserved trait with the *C*, but has nothing in common with the *D*.

And the *C* shares the task-oriented trait with the *D* and the reserved trait with the *S*, but has nothing in common with the *I*.

So it would stand to reason that the style of person with which you have nothing in common will most often be the one that give you the most headaches in life. Working closely with or being near people whose styles are drastically different than ours can be challenging. We may even want to seek validation from someone who shares our style to confirm our opinion that someone else is "difficult." Sometimes simply being armed with the information and possessing the awareness necessary to know the differences, along with a willingness to adapt our style, goes a long way in working with people who seem challenging.

Out of control styles

Everything in the above section is accurate. And it is also true that some people aren't just difficult for us. They are difficult for everyone!

Everybody has a personality. We all have personality traits that naturally serve us well and traits we must manage in given situations. As I mentioned in chapter one, there is such a thing as a healthy versus unhealthy personality. It is important to note that individuals with all four DISC styles can have either of them. There are also people at all points in between. Thus, we might view people on a continuum as represented below.

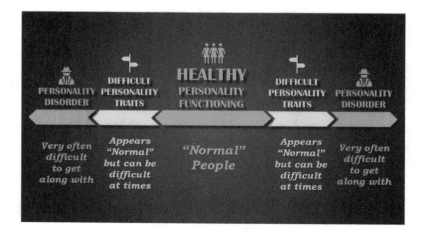

While every one of us falls somewhere on this spectrum and we all have room for personal growth in various areas of our lives, there are people whose styles are what the DISC calls "out of control." These people likely fall in the outer portion of the yellow or all the way in the red. The most extreme of these are actually diagnosable with conditions known as *personality disorders*. Whether or not somebody is fully diagnosable or not is not central to the focus of this book. What is important to know is that the further out on the spectrum a person falls, the more "difficult" they are likely to be.

And it is not just that people are difficult or they are not. You probably know people who are a little bit self-centered, and you also know people who are completely narcissistic. You likely know people who always have to get the last word in edge wise and are stubborn as a mule, but would never hurt a fly. And you may even know of someone who doesn't just have a few "control issues" but whose need to have the upper hand drives them to be abusive.

For instance, "the Bully" (the first type of difficult person we will discuss) represents one version of an out of control **D** and typically has *narcissistic* traits. However, the majority of **D**'s don't fall on one of the red ends of the spectrum. They may have an abundance of self-confidence and slightly less empathy than others, but overall their strengths outweigh their weaknesses.

Suppose you have really acquired training and knowledge in a particular area and have developed some expertise. In that case, it is appropriate for you to have an abundance of self-confidence in that area. However, out of control **D**'s create conflict when they view themselves as experts in multiple areas they aren't experts on, take on arrogant attitudes, and show no regard for the feelings or well-being of others.

Another example would be the Drama Mamma, someone who represents an out of control version of the *I*, and who possesses what clinical language labels *histrionic traits*. This individual is characterized, in part, by overly flirtatious or sexualized behavior, dramatic speech or behavior, and feeling uncomfortable when *not* the center of attention. Having some histrionic traits, (or high amounts of *I*), may be helpful if one is single and trying to attract someone to date or is a motivational speaker wanting to engage a crowd. Being "dramatic" in those specific contexts enhances their ability to be successful in their endeavors. But these traits become obstacle behaviors when their need to get attention drives them to have sex with married coworkers, sing in the middle of a prayer at church, or engage in loud impulsive outbursts at the committee meeting.

So what makes difficult people tick? This is not the title of a psychotherapy book. But let me give you a quick peek behind the curtain to aid in your understanding of difficult people.

The most proven form of therapy is what is called *cognitive behavioral therapy*. This form of treatment was developed by Dr. Aaron Beck at the University of Pennsylvania and others researching in the 1950s and '60s. Beck's research discovered that Sigmund Freud's theory had many flaws (although many therapists and coaches who do not adhere to evidence-based principles still practice from this perspective ignoring all the research). One basic tenet Beck posited that seems elementary today—but was contrary to the Freudian thinking that dominated the psychological landscape at the time—was the idea that *thoughts influence feelings*. Thus, a necessary path to changing emotions involved changing thinking. A simplified, linear version of the model looks like this:

Event → Thoughts → Feelings → Behaviors → Results

So how can cognitive behavioral therapy and coaching inform what is going on with these HC people? What specifically makes their personality styles out of control and why do they behave in ways that cause problems for us? There are several reasons.

Strong beliefs

The Swiss psychiatrist Carl Jung once said, "Until we make the unconscious conscious, it will run our lives and we will call it fate." So where does this unconscious material come from that runs our lives? It comes from our beliefs. It is trendy in coaching circles to say, "Beliefs drive behavior." While this is 100 percent true, 99 percent of people in the personal and professional development space have no idea how this works.

Landau and Goldfried (1923) defined a belief (or schema) as "a mental filter that guides the processing of information." I love this visual. In my experience, just about everyone can identify with the idea of a filter and can formulate an image of how information processing works based on this from one setting or another. Many picture water filters, kitchen appliances, or even oil filters under the hoods of their car. Filters separate certain material out, and funnel other material in. Inserting the "filter" to account for beliefs into Beck's original cognitive model looks like this:

Event ▷ **Thoughts Feelings Behaviors Results**

So when events in life occur (including comments made), we all instantaneously, and usually unconsciously run them through our "filters" that we have in place. This filtering determines what types of thoughts we have—which in turn starts the above cognitive chain most are familiar with.

Some beliefs are completely true, some are completely false, and most are true to one degree or another. Others have nothing to do with truth but are merely opinions or personal preferences. Beliefs can also be helpful or unhelpful.

One of the characteristics of difficult people is that they hold ideas quite firmly. While we might consider it admirable to hold strong convictions in some contexts, it is important to realize *one can believe something with a great degree of conviction and be dead wrong.* And oftentimes rigid thinking becomes problematic in one way or another, particularly in situations where there is no "right" or "wrong." It is common to mistake one's opinion for fact, and many such people cling tightly to beliefs that aren't serving them well.

Last month I was flying back from a speaking tour in Australia. As I boarded my first connection at LAX, I noticed the couple in the seats in front of me was fighting.

The wife said, "Turn the air on, honey."

The husband reached up, rotated the switch, and said, "It won't come on."

"You might have to turn it the other way," her escalating voice responded.

He reached up and gave it a second try. "I'm sorry, I don't think it is on yet."

Yelling at this point, she fired back, "You aren't doing it right—you can't be that stupid!"

They did not talk for the rest of the three-hour flight.

The reality is that the husband was right. The plane was off for refueling and nobody on the plane had access to the air for a short period of time. This example may sound silly, but it does illustrate how a mistaken belief led to conflict-creating behavior that carried over for an extended period of time and made for an unnecessarily tense flight.

So while having strong convictions in certain areas may tell us a lot about a person's character, it is important to recognize the downside of having more fixed attitudes, as they comprise of this unconscious material that drives our behavior outside of our awareness.

Easily triggered

Triggered is a word that you used to only hear in clinical settings but is now making its way into mainstream pop culture. When considering what it means to be triggered, many people have an image of the handle of a gun. We might think of a trigger as something that "sets us off." Colloquially speaking, many of my clients often say things like "so and so really knows how to push my buttons?"

But what are these buttons?

They are our beliefs. So when something happens in life that is connected to the content of one of our specific beliefs, in clinical terms, we say, a belief has been activated. In lay terms, we might say a "button has been pushed," or we have been "triggered."

We all get triggered multiple times every day. For most of us, these are usually minor and often go unnoticed. The more deeply held beliefs a person has, however, the more often they will get triggered and the more intensely they will feel emotions when they do.

Additionally, HC people usually don't just have one strong belief, they may have many. So one way to describe difficult people is to say they have more "buttons" than most people and those buttons are a lot more sensitive than everyone else's. Thus, HC individuals get their buttons pushed more often than most people and get more upset when they do.

Another helpful analogy most of my clients can relate to is comparing their triggers to a bruise. Anyone who has experienced having a bruise knows the deeper the bruise, the lighter the touch on your skin it takes to create a sensation. However, as your bruise begins to heal, you need to use more force to feel discomfort or pain. HC people have many "bruises," and they often go deeper than most, so it feels like you must walk on eggshells to avoid triggering them.

Extreme thinking

As people get triggered, their beliefs immediately produce thoughts specific to that situation. Thought processes can take several forms. One such manifestation is what cognitive behavioral practitioners call *dichotomous thinking*. We might think of this as black-and-white thinking that has no room for gray and keeps people from experiencing middle-ground levels of emotional intensity.

Here are a few examples of dichotomous thinking:

- ♣ "I'm putting it all on the line! I'd rather go to trial and risk losing it all than settle for less than everything!"
- ♣ "Since I didn't ace the test and one person did, I lost. Even though I got the second highest exam score I will never measure up in life."
- ♣ "I had five things planned for the perfect date. If I do what she is suggesting, we will only get to do four of them and the perfect night will be ruined."
- ♣ "It doesn't matter if I am working unauthorized overtime, I have to stay until I get this project completely finished."

You may notice one theme across these mindsets has to do with the extreme language. Certain words or phrases can provide powerful indicators that extreme thinking is occurring. The more we hear this hyperbolic verbiage in others language, or notice it in our own thought life (even if it goes unspoken), the sooner we can identify it as a red flag.

Can you see how this could cause a problem? To the extent that a person engages in this "all-or-nothing" style of thinking, the more difficulty they will have with problem-solving, compromising, and ultimately accomplishing their goals in life. So be on the lookout for phrases like "best ever/worst ever," "never/always," "loves/hates," and so on. The quicker you recognize this, the more time you have to intervene appropriately so you can prevent an interaction from going south.

Intense feelings

Since thoughts always influence feelings, it stands to reason that the more extreme thinking is the more intense emotions will be. Because difficult people have a great degree of conviction in their thinking, whether they are right, wrong, or otherwise, these extreme thoughts always produce emotions felt much more strongly than most people experience feelings.

It is healthy for us all to experience a range of human emotions. Anger, hurt, sadness, fear, guilt are among many emotions that are perfectly healthy for humans to feel in given circumstances. However, when HC people feel angry, they get irate. When they get anxious, they may panic. When they feel disappointed, it crushes them.

Intense emotions can be uncomfortable to be around. They can contribute to low workplace morale, tension in classrooms or courtrooms, and dissension in congregations and boardrooms. Due to these intense emotions, difficult people can "rub their bad off on others." Some say their bad attitudes are uniquely contagious. Similarly, some people, particularly *S's* and *I's* (the people-oriented people) are more vulnerable to having strong emotions if others affect theirs and ruin their day. Nonetheless, intense emotional states are characteristic of people in the "red" area often labelled as "difficult."

Impulsive or inflexible behavior

Extreme thinking and intense emotion lead to impulsive behaviors—and often so quickly you don't see it coming.

This tendency to think or act irrationally makes sense for a couple of reasons. First of all the more *emotionally flooded* (upset) any of us are, the more difficult it is for us to think rationally. We can't process information in the same way that we do when we are in calmer states. While this is true of all of us, because difficult people feel intense emotions much more frequently than everyone else, they are at risk of "not thinking before they act" more often than others.

Think about what it feels like to be upset. It doesn't feel pleasant, does it? It is only natural that humans seek relief from emotional discomfort. Unfortunately, attempts to gain relief or *regulate emotions* often damage relationships, ruin careers, and lead to many other unintended consequences for difficult people.

In summary, we all have *some* of these traits. However, HC individuals lack the flexibility to adapt their behavior depending on what is appropriate for a given context. The reality is that life calls for us to behave differently at a comedy club than we do at a funeral. And for people with difficult personalities, it is as if they can't "be any other way."

Lack of awareness

A final ingredient to the recipe for what makes someone difficult is poor personal insight. So perhaps the worst part of all of this is that not only do individuals with HC personalities behave in all of challenging ways mentioned above, but they do so without realizing they are even doing it! Thus, their behaviors usually become problematic for others before they pose problems for themselves. The challenge in the therapy and coaching world then is that many HC individuals initially have very little interest in being different.

Another type of difficult person the book will discuss is the *Overanalyzer*. This person represents an out of control version of the *C* who has obsessive compulsive personality traits—or is an extreme perfectionist.

A quick note of clarification: This is different than somebody with OCD, which is characterized by behaviors like excessive handwashing, door checking, and other ritualistic or compulsive behaviors or thinking. People with this disorder will often say things like "I know checking the stove nineteen times before I leave the house every time is excessive—I just can't stop!" conversely, people with OCPD (the extreme version of overanalyzers), don't have any awareness that their need for perfection and "completeness" is the reason it is taking them ten times longer than their coworkers to complete a project. They really believe they are doing things the "right" way, and everyone else is just a slob!

Lack of awareness affects several areas. First and possibly foremost, it keeps people from learning from their mistakes. It is popular in today's coaching circles to hear people say things like "fail fast!" or "the key to success is failure!" There was even an article in *Forbes Magazine* in 2018 titled "How to Fail Faster—And Why You Should." If learning were an automatic by-product of failure, then there would be no problem with this approach. However, the problem is that difficult people who lack awareness are missing this critical piece. It is easy for people with healthier personality styles to look at these folks and say, "How in the world could you keep making the same mistake over and over and over!" Without awareness, it is possible to fail time and time and time again and never learn a thing.

Another area affected by lack of awareness has to do with the *assignment of blame.* Do you know one of those chronic apologizers? Those people who are apologizing for everything? Do you think they could really be wrong that often? OK, maybe a few people really are wrong that often! But most of these people constantly moaning *"I'm sorry"* are doing so because their "filter" and lack of awareness of its role impacts their ability to assign blame accurately. Because many people with this style are conflict avoidant, they will often couch it as "taking the high road." **S's** and **I's** are the groups most prone to do this. **D's** and **C's** are the groups most likely to primarily blame others when in reality they are primarily to blame. By the way, those who engage in that black-and-white thinking will be much more likely to say a situation is "all their fault" or "all the other persons fault." Healthier people can do what my teachers often did when I turned my homework in late in school— assign *partial credit.* They can make determinations such as "even though what she did was completely unacceptable, my response also played a small role in escalating the situation." I often hear people say things like "I don't blame anyone. I'm not the judging type." The reality is we all assign blame in our minds based on the circumstances of a situation and our beliefs. Newsflash: Contrary to popular belief, there is nothing wrong with "judging." However, the ability to assign blame or responsibility where it rightfully belongs in different situations is a huge part of what makes more healthy personality styles. People who lack this awareness will continue to be difficult for others until they exhibit some growth.

Now that we have some definitions of some of the general characteristics that can make people difficult, let's dive into the process we will follow on our journey, the specific types of HC people, how to recognize them, what makes them tick and how to disarm the bomb before it detonates!

3

Power with People:
The Blueprint

heesy social media memes challenge people to magically "take back of your power." But very few coaches propagating this advice understand how to facilitate it. So what is the key to truly empowering ourselves so toxic people no longer have the ability to control our environments, moods, and lives? This chapter will lay out the blueprint for walking you through the step-by-step process for dealing with each type of HC person that will be followed in their respective chapters:

1. Identifying red flags.
2. Connecting with them.
3. Acquiring tips for managing them.

4. Speaking their language.
5. Setting boundaries.
6. Enforcing consequences and walking away.

Recognizing "red flags"

I can't tell you how many times I have heard clients utter variations of the line "I don't know what happened to him. It's like he just became a completely different person overnight." Truthfully, this change rarely happens overnight. A traumatic brain injury, the onset of certain medical conditions, or clinical traumas may represent the few exceptions to this rule. Note the use of the term *clinical* trauma. Many people use the term "trauma" colloquially to mean different things. For example, a client said to me recently, *"That relationship was traumatic."* While it is true that all trauma is not created equal, a threshold must be crossed that rises above what most people mean when they use the word "trauma." There is a difference between dealing with a breakup after a six-month relationship and being repeatedly raped.

Regardless, our personality development begins at a very early age. While later life experiences and attachments can contribute to how we change over time, a large portion of "who we are" is already set by adolescence. So when my client made the statement of her boyfriend in his forties that "he just completely changed overnight," the reality was that he had not changed that much at all. He had been like this since the day she met him and hid it from her for a period of time. Actually, he didn't have to put forth much effort because she wasn't looking for it. She was only looking at the traits in him she was enamored with and ignoring anything that could have been considered "red flags" along the way.

The same phenomenon was true for the human resources professional who consulted me.

His first statement was "Jeff, there was no sign he would be like that in his interview." However, once we talked, it became crystal clear there were multiple signs throughout the hiring process that they were likely dealing with a Bully. The HR director was just not seeing them. He was looking for certain qualities the management team wanted, which this individual had in abundance, but did not notice the many red flag traits the candidate possessed as well.

Sometimes this process is more conscious than others. It doesn't matter if you are a CEO of a major corporation making organizational decisions or a private citizen considering whether or not to date someone in your personal life. This mistake of being so laser-focused on the qualities we *do want* that we completely miss the traits we *don't want* comes in three flavors:

♣ The person is completely *unaware* of the weaknesses that often accompany a given set of strengths, so they simply don't know what to look for. Or, even worse, they don't know they should look at all! People who lack the understanding that there is a science to human behavior miss the fact that traits often clump together, and that you can easily identify specific red flags if you know what to look for.

♣ The person has an idea of the weakness that can accompany a given set of strengths but is simply *unintentionally focused* on positive traits and completely misses the negative red flags altogether. As our world evolves in its levels of political correctness, non-judgmentalism and acceptance continue to be increasingly prioritized. A by-product of this has been an explosion of the strength-based movement. While this emphasis has many benefits, one drawback is that those who take it to an extreme lose their critical thinking abilities. The reality is that we *have* to make judgements about what is "good" or "bad," "healthy" or "unhealthy," "effective" or "ineffective" to make the best personal or professional decisions to serve our personal or organizational interests. Unfortunately, some people have become so focused on not judging that they focus on the strengths to the detriment of missing obvious red flags.

♣ The person knows the red flags and even notices several of them, but consciously chooses to ignore them while focusing on the admirable traits they want to see. Many people I work with attend denominations of churches that teach variations of the "believe it and it will happen" doctrine. This positive confession mentality creates an aversion to being honest about negative realities in their life. A mother in this particular faith-based group told me in a recent conversation, "I have just been praying for his behavior at school so hard and believing for it, so the first three times the principle called I just knew it had to be those bad kids picking on him again." Similarly, once I took a deeper dive with my client who believed her boyfriend had "changed overnight," she acknowledged several times she "ignored it hoping it wasn't what I thought." Red flags almost always exist whether we have the capability of spotting them or not. So it is in our best interest to get good at noticing them.

Connecting

In his book *Everyone Communicates, Few Connect, The New York Times* best-selling author John C. Maxwell highlights a phenomenon that may seem obvious, but that never ceases to amaze me: The degree to which people have difficulty genuinely connecting with others. Studies suggest that social media may be contributing to this reality growing in prevalence. Maxwell cites that the average person receives thirty thousand messages per day and speaks sixteen thousand words per day. If you transcribe those words, it would fill up a three-hundred-page book every day! With all of the practice we have sending and receiving messages, it is hard to believe we still struggle with this so much. Even with all the information available these days, how many still struggle to find a healthy significant other, relate effectively with coworkers, or even connect in a meaningful way with friends?

Just because one person is talking and the other who is physically present "hears" them doesn't mean they are genuinely listening or the message hits its mark. Likely everyone reading this book has had the experience of going to great lengths to explain something only to feel misunderstood.

This misunderstanding conjures up an image for me of sitting in the Miami airport one time following a series of speaking and coaching engagements. I remember distinctly noticing the noise and how loud it was, even compared to the many other experiences I already had in airports. Looking around, I tried to pinpoint what was happening around me that contributed to all the "noise." I noticed four specific conversations happening in my vicinity, all of which were happening in Spanish! At that moment my experience struck me as a powerful metaphor that has stuck with me years after it was over. Although I heard multiple voices and a lot of words being spoken, it was all just "noise" as far as I was concerned, none of which registered with me.

I was reminded of this when conversing with a man who was head of his sales team. This gentleman, a self-proclaimed "high *D*," described one of his employees, Zach, who had a lot of *I* in his style, walking into his office and talking for thirty minutes about people he had on his list to sell to. When Zach left, he said, "We had a great talk—we talked about a lot of potential clients!" The manager's response was quite different: "That's thirty minutes of my life I'll never get back—he hasn't sold anything to even one of them!" While Zach walked away feeling optimistic about the interaction, he had no insight into how his manager perceived the conversation—because they didn't speak the same language. In both scenarios, many words were spoken, but very few hit their mark and achieved their desired intent.

The more trust, mutual respect and even emotional attachment we have with a person, the greater the influence we'll have over their decisions. This is true in all types of relationships: romantic relationships, friendships, student-teacher relationships, manager-employee relationships, clergy-parishioner relationships, and buyer-seller relationships, just to name a few. Thus, connecting is a foundational element of communicating effectively with anyone. And this truth is only amplified when it comes to dealing with difficult people.

While future chapters will take a deeper dive into connecting strategies for different types of HC people, consider the following general strategies that apply to all individuals.

- ♣ **Connect on common ground**—This principle works with every personality style. Thus, the more observant among you will note this is the first tip for connecting with each of the specific types of difficult people addressed in this book. You may have four thousand differences (I know, a little Drama Mamma there), but look for what you have in common. One shared interest, hobby, or cause can go a long way. For example, I once partnered with an international nonprofit group for a few years. While the director and I perhaps literally had nothing else in common, we shared a desire to help this particular marginalized group of society. And when I say nothing, I mean nothing. If I made a list of my top ten values, hobbies, and interests, this lady literally would have zero of the same ones on her list. But by finding one element of common ground, we harnessed our shared passion in this one area to enrich many people's lives.

♣ **Add value**—This phrase has been so overused in the leadership and coaching world it has almost lost its meaning. However, among all the self-centered, inwardly focused people in this world, truly offering to serve someone else stands out from the crowd. It can be a small thing, but identify something you think will truly benefit the other person and go out of your way to offer it. You may be surprised how much of an impact it makes on someone.

♣ **Be real**—Some of my clients say they find it unnecessary to make this point. However, today's society is chock-full of people putting on facades. Many people are too insecure to make themselves vulnerable. Others see connecting simply as a means to an end (i.e., the salesperson who wants to "connect" so they can sell them or the "teacher's pet" who "connects" with the teacher so as to win favor in their eyes). While it is true that a good majority of our actions come out of mixed motives, make an honest attempt to be yourself. You might surprise someone.

♣ **Go for an eight-second ride**—In bull riding circles, this phrase (also a popular country music song) refers to the length of time the cowboy needs to stay on his bull for the ride to "qualify." As it relates to this book, seven to eight seconds has been found to be the estimated length of time it takes to make a first impression. Although many claim they don't make judgments, the reality is that we all do—and research has shown typically within seven to eight seconds. Furthermore, we all know you don't get a second chance to make a first impression. The point? Get to the point. Be especially cognizant of how you come across in your initial interactions with people. It will likely make or break your ability to connect with them.

♣ **Practice active listening.** One way to make that first impression you desire sounds incredibly simple, but is actually very difficult for many today. It involves listening. Really listening. Psychology undergraduate and even some early graduate programs teach what they call "active listening" in courses. To this day, it amazes me that people need classes to teach them how to listen. But some people cannot just offer congruent responses. I actually had one fellow student in a counseling course who epitomized this problem. In his attempt to implement what he learned in class in his therapy sessions, he inadvertently accentuated his connection problem. In a supervised therapy session (where several of us in the class observed an actual therapy session of his from behind a one-way mirror), I observed the following.

Client: (crying) "I can't believe he is gone. A parent is not supposed to outlive their children. Twelve years old is far too young. He didn't even get to live his life."

Student therapist: (in an energetic voice with loud volume and excited mood) "Very interesting!"

The response (although a phrase suggested in one of the active listening textbooks) was completely incongruent with the painful event the patient had just exhibited the vulnerability and trust to share!

Similarly, in a later session with a different patient, I observed:

Client: (in an excited voice) "I am so pumped! When I got the letter and opened it up, I saw first thing I had been accepted. I never thought I would get to go to college!"

Student therapist: (in monotone expressionless reply): "Yes, go on."

These are extreme examples, but from an individual who went on to become a licensed psychotherapist! And unfortunately, this case is not the exception in the behavioral health world.

Listen intently. "Feel" their mood. Reflect their words to let them know you hear them and are with them. But don't be a robot. And don't be a weirdo.

- ♣ **Learn to become empathetic.** One way to let them know you "feel" where they are coming from and thereby make the first impression you want is to practice empathy. Some people are naturally better at this than others. Empathy can be developed, but not easily. An academy of cognitive therapy colleague of mine (Chris Padesky) likes to say, "People have good reasons for behaving badly." Some hear this as excusing bad behavior. Practicing empathy doesn't mean making excuses for the person. Sometimes, as this book will discuss, consequences and discipline are appropriate. And sometimes direct words need to be said. However, empathy helps us have a more compassionate heart, and likely take a more effective approach *as* we say what we need to say. I remember my grandad saying it was hard to hate a man once you have heard his story. We would do well to remind ourselves when dealing with HC people that if we were born with their mother and their father and had their siblings, or were made to go stay with their babysitter we may have learned to come across in ways that they are. And if we had their background, socioeconomic status, their teachers and some of their past experiences ... perhaps we would have turned out similar? Do everything you can to put yourselves in their shoes. It will help you connect with them versus set up an adversarial tone.

Tips for dealing with difficult people

After identifying red flags and attempting to connect with the person, the next step is dealing with them strategically. Each chapter will give a "top ten" list of tips for dealing with that particular type of difficult person, considering their unique mindset and behavioral tendencies. This "blueprint" chapter will offer ten general strategies for dealing with all HC people.

1. **Connect before all else**. Spoken to above. Although connecting will not guarantee that you WILL be effective with people, failure to connect guarantees that you will NOT be effective with them.
2. **Get them on board**. The days of the bullying management team are coming to an end. Many people

don't like to be told what to do. While a big part of leadership is making important decisions and giving directives, collaborating with people and soliciting their input is generally much more effective than giving an order that, even if complied with, fosters resentment. Most people are much more likely to work hard for people they like.

3. **Use neutral, non-blaming language**. Saying things like "I hope there are no hard feelings" is a way to stay Switzerland. By using language like this in your interactions you don't assign the blame to them, which will immediately put them on the defensive, yet you also don't enable their mindset by shifting responsibility off of them. Even if you know an event or interaction went poorly because of their behavior, using this language keeps the door open for you to have a necessary conversation. The minute they feel accused, you slam the door shut.

4. **Assign positive meaning to their actions**. Like the tip above, even if you believe they *did* have ulterior motives, this disarming technique of communicating that you assume they have the best intentions stops them in their tracks. "You have to be a person who cares deeply—if you weren't so concerned with the well-being of the organization and its people, I'm sure you wouldn't be pointing out people's mistakes so often. If nobody ever brought these to our awareness none of us could ever improve." Very few will respond to this statement by escalating, and even the most persistent challengers will often sink into silence. Look for and communicate positive intent behind their behaviors. Even if that was *not* their true motivation, nobody will argue back with you

to essentially say "wait—you are wrong—I do NOT have noble intentions!"

5. **Examine expectations**. This is an idea you will hear throughout the book. It is related to what in cognitive therapy and coaching circles we call "*should statements.*" When we expect people to behave in certain ways and then don't, our internal dialogue says things like "*She shouldn't do this, or he shouldn't do that.*" "*Supposed to,*" "*ought to,*" "*needs to,*" "*has to*" *and* "*must*" are among the many shoulds in disguise. Once we understand a person's behavioral profile, it is irrational for us to expect people to behave in ways that are contrary to their character or established patterns of behavior. For instance, it doesn't make any sense for us to expect a Bully to show empathy. It is almost crazy for us to expect someone who always asks for help to make an independent decision. It is unreasonable for us to expect someone who is obsessive-compulsive to give up their anal nature to estimate something and call it "good enough." When we shift our expectations of others, we take back a lot of emotional peace when dealing with them.

6. **Beat the dead horse!** Being raised on a farm and growing up with horses, I never liked this expression. But it has been around for centuries and has to do with revisiting a subject or topic repeatedly. This is one of the most basic principles of behaviorism. Once we have a connection with a person and a mutual agreement to attack a problem behavior, point it out. Notice it. Bring it up. Again. And again. And again. The more we pay attention to a given behavior the more it almost magically changes on its own.

7. **Don't feed into their negativity.** As with many of the principles discussed in this book and accompanying training and coaching programs, this is easier said than done. But when being surrounded by negativity of different kinds, it can be easy to over-identify with the plight of their struggle. Keep an objective mind. Talk with other people who see it differently. Validate their pain without letting their emotional upset rub off on you.

8. **Identify and harness their strengths.** Strengths don't get too much run in a book devoted to dealing with challenging behaviors that drive us nuts. However, even though it takes more than emphasizing strengths when dealing with HC individuals, it doesn't mean this can't be a powerful component of working with them. Everyone has value. All people have gifts, strengths, and talents. As will be addressed, every personality trait is a double-edged sword. Because HC individuals have out of control traits they get labeled as "weak." And they are when they cause problems for themselves or others. But remember, each of these "weaknesses" is rooted in a "strength." If we can help them find that inherent quality and help them dial the out of control trait back a little—or sometimes even find a context in life that it is helpful—we can redirect the trait and use its power for good not evil!

9. **Go above their heads.** Most of us don't like doing this. And it should always be a last resort. But with some people it is the only way to protect ourselves. Go to management. Consult clergy. Get a restraining order. Email a school administrator or school board member. Bring in a third party. With some people in some situations, bringing a little leverage to bear

on the person meaningful to them is the only way to influence change.

10. **Bring in the reinforcements!** Once people change and begin to exhibit the desired behavior, point it out! Oftentimes people actually do start to change but others are so conditioned to see them though their old lens that the positive change in behavior is not reinforced. Sometimes, people are even invested in others being the "bad guy" that they keep looking for the "evidence" they have not changed. I often work with clients who used to exhibit a negative behavior ten times out of ten when they got the chance—but through coaching, therapy and hard work on their part, have changed dramatically—and now are only doing the negative behavior one time out of ten—but the spouse, supervisor, or teacher continues to highlight the one misstep and ignore the nine successes. Learn to view progress differently. Notice even the smallest legitimate steps in the right direction. Praise them. Reinforce the changes in ways meaningful to them. Be a part of their continued development. You will both feel like a part of the process and the outcome will be gratifying for all.

Speak their language

In the same way that I might want to learn Spanish if I make future plans to visit the Miami airport again, Zach could benefit immensely from knowing he has a lot of *I* in his personality style and that his boss is a "high *D*." You may have heard communication defined as *"a message sent plus a message received."* I love this definition. It gives us a "recipe" of sorts, which can provide a visual formula for understanding how to talk to difficult people.

Communication = message sent + message received

It is crucial to recognize that the beliefs, or the way we "filter" information, play a vital role in the *sending* and *receiving* parts of this equation. Take for instance the employee I worked with whose personality style was as an **S**, who approached her supervisor to request time off. Knowing that **S's** have beliefs related to the idea that "sacrificing is always best," how might you guess that affected the language she used when she made the request?

Here is essentially what she said:

"I was wondering, if it's not too much trouble, if there would be a time that was convenient in the next month for me to take a couple of days off? I know everybody is working really hard, so I almost hate to ask ... But I am really starting to feel run-down."

Can you see how her belief "filtered" the language she used? When we diagramed it for her in a coaching session, it looked like this.

Event	Belief	Words ("Sending")
Asking for time off	"Sacraficing is always Best"	"I was wondering, if it's not too much trouble, if there would be a time that was convenient in the next month for me to take a couple of days off? I know everybody is working really hard, so I almost hate to ask ... But I am really starting to feel run-down."

From this mapping, she could understand immediately the role her belief played in the "sending" of the message.

How would you guess her supervisor received this? It depends on the personality style of the supervisor of course. If his style were also an **S**, the "receiving," filtering it through a similar belief, would likely look like this:

Event	Belief	Thoughts ("Receiving")
Employee asks for time off saying … I was wondering, if it's not too much trouble, if there would be a time that was convenient in the next month for me to take a couple of days off? I know everybody is working really hard so I almost hate to ask … But I am really starting to feel run-down."	"Sacraficing is always Best"	"How thoughtful of her to be so considerate of the team. She definitely deserves it. I will give it to her, even if it means I have to work a few more hours."

However, if her supervisor had a *C* style, the response would have been quite different. Likely something like this:

Event	Belief	Thoughts ("Receiving")
Employee asks for time off saying ... I was wondering, if it's not too much trouble, if there would be a time that was convenient in the next month for me to take a couple of days off? I know everybody is working really hard so I almost hate to ask ... But I am really starting to feel run-down."	"Sacraficing is always Best"	"Sure she can have it, but only after the current project is complete and only if it doesn't conflict with existing calendar bookings—I'll need to go over the schedule again just to make sure and then I'll get back to her after I am certain."

With this in mind, when trying to reason with unreasonable people, it can be helpful to ask the following five questions:

1. Who am I?
2. Who are they?
3. Who are they to me?
4. Who am I to them?
5. How do I talk so they will listen?

Let's look at the significance of each.

1. Who am I?

Awareness is one of the themes in this book. One of the crucial skills you will learn in the pages that follow is how to *adapt* your verbiage used to "speak the language" of the person you are talking to in order to increase the likelihood of having a successful interaction. Having an awareness of who we are is of the utmost importance in this regard, because if we do not know our style, we don't know our baseline we have to *adapt* from.

If you have not taken a basic DISC assessment within the past year, I highly recommend doing so. You can take your assessment at ***bit.ly/DrRasmt.*** You will refer to your assessment results throughout the rest of the book or coaching program if you are participating in that.

Taking this assessment is one way to, as CG Jung put it, "make the unconscious conscious." Knowing your style will give you powerful insight into the language you use without even realizing it. Until we gain at least a moderate level of this awareness, our speech patterns just flow out of our mouths on "autopilot." For example, how often have you heard people say variations of "he just doesn't have a filter!" The reality is that we all have filters. These determine the words that come out of our mouths until we acquire the skills to turn off our "autopilots," observe the language we use, and strategically adapt that based on who we are talking to and the goals we have.

So dealing with difficult people all starts with awareness. We cannot fix what we don't perceive as broken. Learn your style, so you will know what "autopilot" tendencies you need to guard against in your communication. Otherwise, your efforts to use the forthcoming strategies to deal with the different types of HC people you will encounter will likely be fruitless.

2. Who are they?

Now that you have identified your own style you are off to a great start! The next step is to get better at recognizing the styles of other people. It can be helpful to start with the styles of people you have *no* real need to understand. Let them be "practice." Observe family members. Watch conversations in the restaurant. Look for it in sitcoms. Before long, these traits will just jump out at you and you won't have to look that hard. Then identify one difficult person. Look for the signs described in this book. Remember we are all a unique blend of each of the four general styles. Still, the more "out of control" a person's emotions, behaviors and traits appear, the less blurry the lines will be. You will be able to identify them more accurately. And hopefully sooner in the process now that you are armed with in-depth knowledge. Identifying "who they are," will give you powerful insight into the language you need to use for your message to "hit the mark."

3. Who are they to me? This one gets a little trickier. But don't be intimidated.

Defining ourselves in terms of our relationship to another person is something most of us do without even recognizing it. A client once brought his wife to a session and introduced her as his "better half." At a parent-teacher conference, a five-foot-three petite woman named "Miss Sonya" once introduced me to a six-foot-five muscular man by proudly gushing, "He will always be my little brother."

Simply think about who you are. Based on your style of thinking, what perceptions do you have of people with the different styles? The chart below has served as a helpful resource for understanding tendencies.

Styles	Perception
D to D	"They mean business too! Let's go!"
D to I	"They need to calm down and get down to business."
D to S	"They need to stop talking and get down to business."
D to C	"The need to speed things up and get with it."
I to D	"They need to have some fun!"
I to I	"They are fun too! I like them!
I to S	"They need to come out of their shell!"
I to C	"They need to lighten up big-time!"
S to D	"They need to be more sensitive."
S to I	"They are fun but need to tone it down."
S to S	"They care about feelings too!"
S to C	"They are cold and unsupportive."
C to D	"They need to slow down and get it right."
C to I	"They need to be more serious."
C to S	"They need to stop talking and focus."
C to C	"They attend to detail like they should."

For instance, if your style has a lot of *S* in it and you are talking to a *D*, *to you*, they may be "intimidating," "mean," and "abrasive." Know that if your autopilot takes over, you are likely to cower down, lose assertiveness, and sabotage yourself from getting what you want out of the interaction.

Or, if your style is high in *C* and you are preparing to talk to someone with a fair bit of *I*, *to you* they may be "boisterous," "flamboyant, "and "annoying." With this knowledge of how your perception colors the thoughts and feelings you will likely have with them during the interaction, you can better prepare for more emotionality than you are likely comfortable with. Knowing what to expect ahead of time can prepare you to summon a little extra portion of patience, give you an increased readiness to pin them down on some details, and minimize the drama.

So as we discuss each type of difficult person, which represents an "out of control" version of one of the four DISC styles, you will need to consider the question, *"Who are they to me?"* *to* better prepare you for counteracting *your* tendencies when dealing with that particular difficult style.

4. Who am I to them?

This question asks you to put on your empathy hat. If your style has a lot of *D* in it, this may not come naturally to you, but it is a good exercise for all of us, nonetheless. Put yourself in their shoes. More accurately, put yourself in their head. Scary thought? Perhaps. But it is an integral part of adopting an intentional approach to dealing with difficult people.

The table above may help you consider this question as well. You have a strategic advantage by knowing how they will view you and how they are likely to interact with you because of their perceptions.

For instance, if your personality style is high in the *C* trait and you plan to engage someone with elevated qualities of the *D*, you know ahead of time that *to them* you are slow, too detail oriented, and perhaps "anal." Based on this, you can anticipate they will likely want you to move faster, compromise quality, and not "sweat the small stuff."

On the contrary, if your style contains high *D* traits and you are preparing to have a chat with someone largely in the *C* category, you can assume ahead of time that *to them*, you are a bulldog who takes charge and runs over people, not taking adequate time to do things the way they "should" be done. Based on this you know ahead of time they will likely have tons of questions, object to the deadline you want to set, and demand to hear what quality checks you have put in place. Knowing this ahead of time can arm you to approach a meeting ready to exercise your patience, prepare with details you might not ordinarily have, and read to move more slowly than your autopilot wants to. Armed with these style-specific tools you will be much more prepared to accomplish the task at hand.

So as we discuss each type of difficult person you will also need to consider the question, *"Who am I to them?"* Understanding this can help you better prepare you to "read" them accurately so you can use the language necessary to disarm that particular difficult person.

5. How do I need to adapt to speak their language?

The final piece of this puzzle involves asking the question, "How do I need to alter my communication to be sure my message hits the mark with this particular person?"

I often think about the evening I invited the husband of one of my clients to join us for a session.

He emphatically asked me, "She is the only person in the world who would have taken what I said in that way. Why should I have to walk on eggshells and change every word I say when no one else on the planet would have taken it like that!"

My response was simple. "Because you aren't married to anyone else on the planet."

Remember, the secret reminds us that the criteria for communicating with others cannot rely on our feelings, beliefs, or how we think something or someone *should* interpret something. When the reality of how they *currently do* interpret information deviates significantly from our expectations of how we think it "should," our communication is likely dead on arrival. In many cases, the other person could benefit from working on their "receiving." Perhaps they already are or need a referral to a coach or a counselor. But that is usually not your role. (Unless you are their supervisor or leader in some capacity.) And until that person can change how they think and react, we need to deal with the realities of their *current* personality styles.

My answer to him continued. "The reality is you are married to her. The reality is that this is how she currently takes things. We are working on her perceptions and her responses and I am confident, with time, she will make many changes you will like. But until I can help her progress in those areas, she will continue to interpret your comments of that nature in that way every time. Every. Single. Time. So why do you have to change how you say things? You don't. You are an adult. This is America. You can respond in whatever way you choose to. But just know that every time you choose to say things the way you did, until she makes some of these changes I mentioned, I just want you to know that you will continue to get this exact same reaction."

Many people like to quote Gandhi's "Be the change you want to see," but few actually practice it in relationships. We must be willing to see our role in the problem and be flexible enough to adapt our strategy if we want to be part of the solution.

If you don't, you will be speaking Spanish to me in Miami.

Talking so people will listen

According to the old English dictionary, "one can hear without even trying to." Listening, however, requires intentional and sustained effort. Millions of people hear. Very few listen. And, as many wives will attest to, it is also possible to pretend one is listening when all they are doing is hearing.

In the early 1990s, actor and comedian Martin Lawrence popularized the phrase "talk to the hand!" This phrase, frequently accompanied by a gesture of obstinately putting one's hand up with a straight arm, became a trendy way of dismissing someone, essentially saying, "You can keep talking, but I am not listening."

This attitude often reflects the stance of many types of difficult people. It is, in fact, one of the aspects that makes them difficult. People often feel like they are "talking to the hand." So how do we talk in a way that even these people will listen?

We "talk to the belief." Or to the "filter" we know they have because of their style. At a deeper psychological level than basic DISC material will teach, this is what it really means to understand how to speak people's language. This principle is true for communicating with everyone, but with difficult people it is of utmost importance. Why? Because as referenced in chapter 2, their "filter" is not the same size as everyone else's. Thus when communicating with them there is less margin for error; they are more easily triggered, so we need to be more precise with our language.

John C Maxwell asked the question, "How do we make sure our message hits the mark?"

For me this always elicits the image of a target. The closest I ever got to a target was the dartboard in my basement growing up. But one of my clients was proficient in archery, and this was powerful imagery for him. I think it can be beneficial for any of us.

To follow the metaphor, many people in life are what we might call "laid-back," or "easygoing." We can hit "anywhere on the target" with many of them, and our message will "get through" effectively. But for difficult people, we must hit the exact bullseye, or we will likely trigger them. When this happens, we would be well advised to beware of getting hit by the shrapnel flying from the explosion likely to ensue.

The chapters that follow will help you learn to hone your language to "get through" to eight of the most difficult types of people encountered all over the world. Ninety-nine percent of communication "experts" don't realize the two essential ingredients when approaching unreasonable people. First, the *content* must be specific to the type of difficult person you are dealing with and will be addressed in the upcoming chapters. Secondly there is the *process*.

For years, people would ask me a version of the question, "Dr. Riggenbach, how are you so good at dealing with these people who drive everyone else nuts!"

While I had a few ideas, the reality was I didn't quite know the answer to that question. I knew I was doing a combination of what I was trained to do and what I intuitively understood about how to implement it, but I couldn't put it into words. I have always heard, "If you can't teach it to someone else, you don't *really* know it."

So I took up the challenge, and began observing myself. I first paid attention to the language I used, noticing the order I used it in. And I made note of my "playbook" for how to respond when things went well and when things went poorly. Here is a brief summary of my findings.

First, I always validated before doing or saying *anything* else. My academy of cognitive therapy colleague Bob Leahy says, "Not everyone is ready to change, but everyone is ready to be validated." I have found this to be true. There is an expression I heard many years ago that I have found helpful: "Validation is the WD-40 of change." Most of us, as humans, need to "loosen up" a little before we are ready to move forward. In sales a version of this might be akin to "warming the prospect." Validation provides an internal comfort or safe spot where a person feels understood enough to move forward into action within the environment created.

We know from brain research that any time we as people become emotionally overwhelmed, we lose our capacity to process information in the same way we typically do. One coaching client told me "I was so worked up I couldn't think straight!" Some of the newer techniques in cognitive therapy aim to manipulate what we refer to as a patient's *affect* or observable mood. Techniques to "quiet the amygdala" help reduce escalated emotion into the range it needs to be to produce the most profound changes in their thinking. As non-clinicians dealing with people in everyday life, it can still be tremendously helpful to find ways to decrease a person's emotional intensity to help them calm down before attempting to have an important conversation or give a directive. Validating represents one powerful yet simple way to do this.

Additionally, I noticed my validation was not generic in nature. The "active listening" taught in many graduate schools for behavioral health professionals is maddening. Many of my clinical clients described leaving psychologists or other behavioral health providers because of variations of the complaint "She just kept repeating what I said and saying things like 'That must have been hard.' I wanted to scream back at them, '*OF COURSE IT WAS HARD. THAT'S WHY I'M HERE!*'"

I also noticed I was speaking directly to the person's situation and their perception of it (or to their filters). So, to people who had experienced deep hurt in their past I found myself saying "I can't even imagine how vulnerable it must make you feel." And to people who had been taken advantage of in the past I caught myself saying, "Based on what you have been through, I don't blame you at all for being a little suspicious—shoot, I wouldn't trust me either if I were you!"

As I began to practice this more intentionally, I was amazed at the power it had to get through to people.

The next thing I observed I would do was to *clarify my intent*. Remember, our filters distort information based on our experiences and the meaning we assign to them. So if I knew the person felt unsafe, I would go out of my way to clarify that *in the present moment* they were safe. Similarly, if I knew the person had beliefs based on their past related to others being untrustworthy, I emphasized where I was coming from and offered assurance that they would not be taken advantage of in the present situation.

The final step in my communication was simply asking for what I wanted from them—whether that involved completing a homework assignment, having a conversation with someone, or doing an aspect of a project that needed to be completed.

Since everyone has an acronym these days and I have a lot of *S* in me and want to fit in, I developed this simple "formula" summarizing what I had learned from myself.

I've never been good at acronyms, but Batman taught me that the best way to disarm an attacking foe always involved a good BAM. So here it is:

B is for **B**elief-based validation. While everyone else is talking to the hand, talk to the belief. Apply the WD-40 and prepare for the ask.

A is for **A**ffirming your true intentions. Offering this clarification from the beginning serves as a "preemptive strike" of sorts. That is, you immediately counteract objections formulated by their beliefs based on what may have been true in the past but is *not* true in the present situation. These affirmations further help to disarm any potential reactive response.

M is for **M**essage. After and only after you do steps one and two, you are ready to send your message. Make your request. Ask your question. Give your directive. Be clear about your objective in that particular interaction.

For my client who I knew had been hurt in the past, our dialogue in one interaction looked like this.

"Misti, (**B**) I know that you have been hurt a lot in the past and I can't imagine how vulnerable you must feel putting yourself out there, (**A**) and so we are going to offer you a safe place to do it. I want to do everything necessary to be sure you are in control of the process—(**M**) but I need you to be honest with the team about a few things."

See how that worked? This client was known for biting people's heads off. What most failed to realize was because of things that happened in her past nobody knew about, she felt constantly threatened. The "tough girl" front served the purpose of scaring everyone away and keeping them at arm's length. She had almost become proud of what she would call her "bitchy" persona. However, using the BAM, cutting the chaff and speaking directly to her vulnerability immediately disarmed her and stopped her in her tracks. It was as if I said, *I know who you really are. You can save yourself the energy that is required to pretend.* In that interaction, I didn't see one glimpse of the "strong" woman we normally saw. No angry tone of voice. No profanity. No veiled threats. The tough girl melted in front of me and we had a genuine conversation about what needed to happen for her to ensure the best outcome for everyone.

I've included example BAMs in each chapter and you will have an opportunity to formulate your own based on the types of HC people in your life. I will also give you a "top ten" list of tips for handling each specific type of difficult personality.

Setting boundaries and enforcing consequences

The BAM is almost magic. This approach has proven to be highly effective for dealing with almost anybody, no matter how difficult. And still some people don't respond.

I have found that at times, the BAM is close to working, but just needs a little massaging or repeating. If the **M** is not initially complied with, it can be helpful to simply circle back to the **B** and offer additional validation before asking again in a different way. Sometimes just the slightest bit of additional "loosening" is required. It may, however, at some point become necessary to take the extra step of setting a boundary. Many people are good at drawing the proverbial line in the sand; however, boundaries are of little use without consequences. It's often OK to give a second chance, but if you are a person who gives a third or a fourth or a fifth— you are asking to be treated poorly. Many would do well to remember that the use of limits in difficult conversations has less to do with *telling other people what to do* and more about telling them what *we will do* if they don't do what we ask.

I had a client "Sara" who once described a fight with her boyfriend. "I set the boundary with him," she conveyed. "I told him to stop talking disrespectfully to me and to do it now!"

As you may have guessed, this did not go over well and for several reasons.

First, she gave an extremely high **D**, who liked to be in control, an order. Secondly, she was not specific about what she really meant. Contrary to our current cultural understanding, feeling "disrespected" often has more to do with the receiver than the sender, and is inherently subjective. What is disrespectful to one person may be completely different than what is considered disrespectful by another. So even if this guy had any intention of doing what she asked he might not even know what to do. Finally, there was no consequence. So what incentive did he have?

We walked through a few guidelines for setting boundaries that can serve as good reminder questions for all of us when setting boundaries.

1. Be clear about the line.
2. Be clear about the consequence.
3. Be willing to follow through.

We discussed how the conversation could have gone differently if she had used the guidelines and planned how she might address a similar conversation the next time the opportunity inevitably presented itself. She came up with:

"Joe, you know I feel disrespected when you call me names and use profanity. Neither of us will get our points across like this. If you call me another name or use another curse word, I need you to know I'm going to hang up the phone."

Unfortunately (or in some ways fortunately), Sara was given an "opportunity for growth" later that very evening. The good news? When the conversation escalated, as it frequently did, she could say exactly what we had rehearsed.

The bad news? After she said it, Joe continued to yell at her, and she continued to take it.

We often hear that *we teach people how to treat us*. But what does that really mean? And how exactly do we do that?

Sara just did it.

What did she teach Joe about how to treat her in that interaction? If Sara was the teacher, what did Joe, as the student, "learn?"

He put it bluntly in our session later that week: "She doesn't really mean what she says. Between you and me—I can treat her however I want to and the sex will still be there that night."

Setting a boundary, even a clear one, is useless until we follow through.

The rest of the story, by the way, is that Sara did follow through, but only after about six weeks of cognitive coaching. Once we dealt with her ideas related to *"I don't want to be rude," "maybe he will find someone else,"* and *"I can't stand the thought of being without him,"* she could hang up the phone when treated "disrespectfully" and eventually end the relationship.

Sara's case was extreme as her relationship was abusive. Unfortunately, extreme situations often call for extreme actions. However, we can remedy most everyday situations with smaller, less extreme steps that don't necessarily involve ending relationships completely.

Marcy, a mother I once worked with, was incensed her son was not talking to her. When I inquired what precipitated the standoff, I discovered she had grounded him for the entire month. When I asked what he had done, she replied by saying, "He didn't get off his phone and answer me when I asked him a question—he completely ignored me!" We discussed "all-or-nothing" thinking, realistic expectations, and alternative ways to produce the desired behaviors. Although she verbalized that she believed in the theory that "the punishment should fit the crime," her extreme thinking and quickly escalating anger in the moment kept her from generating smaller consequences more appropriate to the line crossed.

In the session that ensued, we identified twenty-five original consequences differing in severity she could use in response to boundary crossings of various kinds. She also discovered over time that using the smaller options in her arsenal more frequently was more effective than allowing multiple misbehaviors to go unaddressed and then eventually blowing up and imposing out of proportion punishments. Not only did she find that approach worked best for changing her son's behavior, but she also realized it worked wonders for her frustration level toward him and helped her feel more compassion as she interacted with him daily.

Know when to walk away, know when to run

Even with all our techniques, we can't stop all people from being jerks. However, we can stop them from being jerks to us. The "right" time to walk away isn't always easy to discern. Inevitably some people have mindsets that cause them to put up with bad behavior for much longer than is good for them. Some never walk away. Some eventually find the courage to, but not before significant damage has been done to them personally, their loved ones, or the organization they are a part of. Unfortunately, excuses such as *"the money is too good,"* or *"I don't want to be seen as intolerant,"* or *"I'll do it when things calm down a bit,"* drive many people to continue to hand the keys to the people who drive them nuts.

Other people are so intolerant of difficult behaviors that they are too quick to pull the trigger. I have seen clients unable to pay their bills, miss opportunities for promotions, and lose children in their classroom for an entire school year because they were unwilling to learn basic skills involved in handling people more effectively.

Seek advice from a coach, friend, or clergy. If you need to, get professional psychotherapy. But undergo the mindset shift that is necessary to, after you have considered the short-term and long-term options, make the tough decision that it is time to pull the plug on the relationship, job, or a staff member. All you can do is all you can do. And once you can say with confidence you have done that, there is great wisdom in walking away.

Each of the ensuing chapters will help you "*know when to walk away*" and "*know when to run*" from each type of difficult person you encounter.

So—that is the basic approach! Now let's dive into what you picked up this book to learn about—the eight types of difficult people and how to deal strategically with each of them before they drive you nuts!

4

The Bully

"I would rather be a little somebody than an evil nobody."

—Abe Lincoln

Beliefs: "I am superior to others / more deserving than others."

Mindset: "Win at all costs, even if a few sensitive people have to be collateral damage."

Behaviors: Ordering others around, yelling, name-calling, threatening

DISC parallel: One out of control version of the *D*

Clinical parallel: A person with *narcissistic personality* traits.

Continuum

Mild	Moderate	Severe
I-----------------------	I-----------------------	I
Direct, "to the point," No validation of feelings	Bossy, demanding demeaning, poor empathy	regularly abuse power, exploit others, emotionally abusive

Description

The Bully represents an out of control version of the *D* prototype on the DISC profile, and in clinical terms, often has *narcissistic* personality traits. It is important to note that many people have some narcissistic traits who are not fully diagnosable with narcissistic personality disorder.

When kept in check, these traits make for excellent leaders. They know how to take charge. They are excellent decision-makers. They are determined, resilient, and productive. They make things happen and get the job done.

On the downside, their intense drive for accomplishment can influence them to be overly direct, demanding, and insensitive to the feelings and needs of others. Sometimes they can also be punitive.

Bullies are known for their name-calling, belittling, ordering people around, and other demeaning behaviors. Even when they don't act that way, they carry themselves with an air of superiority and can come across as quite arrogant. They are "know-it-alls" invested in maintaining their image and have difficulty receiving even constructive criticism.

While most Bullies don't enjoy hurting people, their lack of empathy keeps them recognizing that they do so. They lack patience and need to be admired by other people.

Although deep down, most Bullies are actually quite insecure, they put forth a front that comes across as "tough" and "in charge."

I received a Facebook friend request this week from someone who described herself as an "*entrepreneur, mother, and giver of ZERO f*cks.*" She also had a meme of a Yoda figure saying, "*Care about anything you say I do not.*"

A primary strategy of the Bully is to intimidate. One way to present this front that they are invulnerable involves overt attempts to let you know they don't care what you think. The reality is that they care deeply about what people think. That is why, as we will discuss shortly, they get triggered when their perceived status is not recognized. While it can be hurtful to care what *too many* people think, we stop growing when we get to the point that we don't care what *anybody* thinks. The ability to take constructive criticism is vital for learning and making adjustments necessary to succeed in life. So regardless of how clever these people think they are, while this persona is sending the message that they are tough, what they don't realize is that they are actually screaming "I am insecure!"

Another hallmark quality of someone with these traits is low empathy. Unlike Con Artists, who will take advantage of people and feel no remorse, it is important to realize most Bullies are not without conscience. They usually hurt you or your feelings only if you prevent them from accomplishing their current "mission." So hurting you is not their intent. It is a by-product. Their sin is not that they desire to hurt you—it is that they fail to recognize you. Surprisingly one study looking at physician behavior showed that 80 percent of doctors had no idea their behaviors were being perceived in the way that they were and when made aware, self-corrected. Some victims of Bullies take at least small consolation by gaining this insight. Although their action still hurt you, at least it wasn't personal!

Bullies also believe they are special, "better than," or otherwise different from the norm. By this very definition most people are not special otherwise special would not mean anything! Because of this, Bullies believe they have a "right" to things other "unspecial" people do not.

Because people come to overly deserving beliefs about themselves for different reasons, Bullies take forms you may not expect. A wide variety of backgrounds and experiences form the foundation of entitlement-based attitudes. Some examples of such attitudes include:

- ♣ "Because I have an advanced education, I deserve to be respected more than you."
- ♣ "Because I have more money than you, I deserve special privileges."
- ♣ "Because 'my people' (race, ethnicity, religion) were mistreated in the past, I have a right to special benefits today."
- ♣ "Because I was injured or am handicapped, I deserve special privileges."
- ♣ "Because my family lineage has always been privileged, I deserve to be a class above you."

Some of you reading this may believe one or more of the above attitudes at least to some degree. Remember beliefs are sometimes true, sometimes false, often somewhere in between, and other times just a matter of opinion. What one "deserves" in a society is a source of great debate. The point here is that entitlement mindsets can develop from a variety of historical and personal experiences, some of which we may or may not immediately associate with Bullies. And the stronger that entitlement mindset is, the more the

Bully will believe they merit receiving special treatment, get angry when they aren't the beneficiaries of it, and feel justified to do whatever it takes to "get what they deserve." In short, we need to be careful of stereotypes. Bullies come in all shapes and sizes. For many people an overtly arrogant and conceited man in a suit comes to mind. However, few people would think of the lady in the wheelchair who ran over my six-year-old twins at Disney World and then cussed them out and gave them a lecture about yielding to disabled people when they accidentally stood in a handicapped line.

Finally, they say birds of a feather flock together, and this is certainly true with the Bully. Bullies run in packs. They respect people with whom they share a common perception of superiority. A sobering fact is that bullying appears to be on the rise. Unfortunately, our Western society continues to breed new generations with these entitlement-based attitudes. University of Rhode Island professor Paul Harvey is among the many researchers who investigate the generation of individuals born roughly in the 1990s. In contrast to baby boomers, who largely believed "if you work hard, you will eventually have a successful career," millennials, or Gen Yers believe a successful career is out there just waiting for them on a silver platter and "it is up to me to choose which path I want to take." Thus, this generation, in comparison to previous ones, became tremendously optimistic about their careers, ambitions, and life goals while simultaneously having unrealistic expectations about the amount of work typically required to achieve them. It doesn't take a rocket scientist to understand how these, as Harvey puts it, "unrealistic expectations," "strong resistance to negative feedback," and an "inflated view of oneself" might influence workplace attitudes, school behaviors, and interactions in other arenas of life. Thus, situations requiring hard work, everyone being treated the same regardless of background, and considering others' perspectives can trigger Bullies.

Redflags

I have often heard version of "I never saw it coming. He never showed any signs of it!"

While blatant aggression or hostility rarely surfaces before one's status or position in a job or relationship is secure, there are always more subtle ways to spot Bullies, as early as a job interview or a first date, if you know what you *are* and *aren't* looking for. Keep in mind these will look different in different settings. Here are a few things to keep an eye out for.

Red flags for Bullies in the workplace

- ☐ Have they had bullying-related complaints in previous employment? If so, were they substantiated? (If the claims were unproven, this does not rise to the same level as if they had been substantiated but should also be filed away in your mind and not completely dismissed.)
- ☐ Have they had bullying-related complaints in their current job?
- ☐ If there were previous complaints lodged, ask about them and listen for how they are self-described.
- ☐ Do they take any responsibility in problematic interaction(s)?

- ☐ Do they use demeaning or insensitive language to describe others?
- ☐ Do they "name-drop"? There is a fine line between connecting by acknowledging you know mutual people versus trying to gain status in your eyes simply by alleging association with someone else of elevated status.

Describe a scenario in your unit or department where empathy is required and someone failed to show it. Listen carefully to who in the story they identify with and ask how they would respond to it.

Ask at least one feelings related question and listen carefully to how they answer it. Do they joke about "sensitive people?" Are they able to use feeling language? Do they feel badly for less fortunate people?

Red flags for Bullies in schools

- ☐ Do they tell peers or teachers what to do rather than ask?
- ☐ Do they always have to be the one to initiate a game on the playground or in the hallway?
- ☐ How well do they share?
- ☐ If somebody else initiates a game or conversation, will they engage?
- ☐ Monitor tone of voice, especially when they don't get their way.
- ☐ Have you observed signs of verbal aggression, teasing, or name-calling?
- ☐ How well do they respond to instruction?

Red flags for Bullies in personal relationships

- ☐ How do they treat other people in their life? If they treat you like a queen but treat others like crap, they are likely a Bully.
- ☐ Do they name-call, use demeaning terms, etc., even if in a "joking" way?
- ☐ Are they constantly reference their accomplishments or status?
- ☐ Do they always have to "win" disagreements or arguments?
- ☐ Do they name-drop?
- ☐ Can they listen when you talk? Can they put themselves in your shoes?
- ☐ How do they respond when you voice a different opinion?
- ☐ How important is status to their self-image?
- ☐ How do they react when disrespected?

A workplace example

Scott was a manager at a large health-care system. His charismatic personality had enabled him to climb the organizational hierarchy faster than most. He was well-liked by the CEO and HR manager. One day he received a surprising complaint from perhaps his highest performing employee, Fred, who had worked for him for eight years. The complaint centered around a new hire, Ben, reportedly "making it almost unbearable to work here." Specifically, complaints included name-calling, belittling, making fun of, and sharing embarrassing personal details in front of clients. Upon investigation, Scott discovered most of the complaints had validity. He even called a meeting with Ben during which he admitted to the behavior. Although he allegedly "talked to Ben about it," the behavior continued. Scott was reluctant to push the issue because he knew Ben had a family member in the upper echelon of administration, and the HR director did not like to be "burdened" with employee disputes. He was also especially cognizant of his reputation and knew upper management did not like the images portrayed by departments with internal conflict. Scott continued to avoid the issue, showing that his department ran smoothly and efficiently. Fred submitted his resignation three months later.

A church example

Several years ago, a group from a church I attended went on a mission trip to Africa. Although I did not go on this trip, I gave my friend a ride to the church so his car would not be there all week. While hanging out in the parking lot with the crew, it quickly became apparent that one of the single guys in his thirties, "Dan," was especially impressed with his perceived capabilities to embark on such a trip and wanted others to know about it. He strutted boisterously with his shirt off bragging about his previous military-related travel. Every sentence began with "When I was in the coast guard," and ended with a different type of heroic feat he pulled off in some remote location.

As the final bags were being packed in the last vehicle of the caravan before heading to the airport, I heard a distinct voice making fun of one of the other members of the mission team for the size of her suitcase. He again proceeded to brag about his "experience" with these types of trips, and in a smug, arrogant voice, as he raised his one duffel bag, said, "I know what I need, and what I don't need."

While that marks the end of what I witnessed, what I heard from my friend blew my mind. Apparently, the grizzled coast guard veteran did not bring nearly enough clothes and asked my friend to borrow a shirt by day four. He was so demanding that the people in that remote Tanzanian village ended up firing up their local generator they normally self-rationed to once a month just so the fearless warrior who belittled others in the parking lot could do a load of laundry!

Connecting with the Bully

If you can connect with Bullies, you should. It is much better to have a rapport with this group than to be on their bad side. The following strategies can be helpful when trying to connect specifically with the Bully:

❖ **Compliment them on their accomplishments**. Genuine complimenting is always essential when connecting with someone. The real power comes, however, when complimenting a person related to something they consider meaningful. So remember for Bullies their status or perceived status typically comes from some kind of accomplishment. Clients have questioned my suggestions to compliment Bullies. "I don't want to encourage bad behavior," one man said. However, it is possible to genuinely compliment an accomplishment without condoning all the behavior that went into achieving it. Together, we brainstormed ways for him to compliment a disliked coworker in a comfortable way. The fruit of our labor yielded a response that sounded something like "I can't believe you were salesperson of the year—you were selected over three hundred other people! That is quite an award. I know you put in a lot of hours to make that happen. I admire your work ethic." This tactic compliments what is commendable without addressing their undesirable behavior. In this case, my client was an equal to this "Bully." Not being his superior, it was not his job to be critical of aspects of his performance the rest of the team found dishonorable. In fact, this guy already had multiple complaints filed against him by employees from various departments and levels of authority. While if those behaviors rose to a certain level, it may have become necessary to report them to a supervisor again, the goal of this interaction was to continue to connect with the coworker in a way that kept him from being a target of bullying behaviors that contributed to the hostile workplace environment while he was looking for better employment opportunities.

❖ **Trick them into believing you are special too**. The word "trick" is used a bit facetiously here, because we all are special in our own ways. But if you can get the Bully to view you as part of their exclusive mutual admiration society, they will treat you differently. When this happens, your "specialness" in their eyes creates immediate influence. If you have an elite skill, talent, or remarkable achievement, allowing the Bully to see that can win you points toward connecting with them.

❖ **Get them to believe they are part of something special**. In 2017, after many disappointing seasons under Charlie Strong, Tom Herman took over the Texas Longhorns football program. The change fostered immediate optimism, and according to some recruiting services, and the team garnered the number one recruiting class in the nation. Many coaches and fans who follow recruiting closely wondered how Tom Herman could have gotten such a strong recruiting class his first year. When asked why he chose Texas over several other national powers, one recruit said, "Coach Herman is building something special—Texas is going to start winning championships again and I am going to be a part of something special starting this year. We are going to make history!" The reality is that Texas had a record of seven wins, six losses that year (and the following year), finishing sixth in its own conference and did not even finish in the top twenty-five rankings. Furthermore, Texas has not even won one conference championship in the last decade, let alone been in contention for a national championship. Even though the reality had not come close to matching the "hype," that player, and many others in the class, *believed* they were part of something noteworthy. Once the player bought into that belief, the coaches had immediate influence over his decision-making.

❖ **Use nicknames that recognize their status.** All these connecting strategies are specific to the Bully's cognitive profile. And remember individuals with this style believe they are special for a reason. Reinforcing that reason in simple everyday language can be a powerful way to connect that increases your influence. For example, a former supervisor of mine took enormous pride in his position of status at a reputable hospital. Playfully referring to him as "Bossman" was a way of stroking his ego daily while working to connect with him on common ground. As other employees caught on, he eventually had an entire department using this affectionately subjugating language that he found quite endearing. Those who regularly acknowledged his authority in this simple way won favor in his eye and always had his ear when major decisions were about to come down.

Similarly, I attended a faith-based group for several years with a man who was simply known as "Doc Brown." (he wasn't in *Back to the Future*). Although I also have my PhD, I attended this group for a year without anyone knowing it. Two others in the group were medical doctors (MDs). However, this was such an important part of his identity that he had others calling him "Doc" in a personal group. And he felt "disrespected" when someone did not address him in this manner.

There are three common responses to Bullies: (1) fight back, (2) run away, (3) shut down. None of these will get you what you want. Here are ten tips for dealing with Bullies.

Top ten tips for dealing with Bullies

Disclaimer: How to best respond to a Bully varies significantly depending on context and your relationship to them. I wrote these tips specifically for people in leadership.

1. **Know their triggers and avoid them**. Criticism, rejection, and failure trigger Bullies. If it is not your job to criticize them, refrain. If you are in a position that requires it, choose your words wisely. If absolutely necessary, offer constructive suggestions only after a good dose of validation regarding their significance. Find ways to make them feel special, even while making your point, and always do so privately.

2. **Feed their need to succeed**. Provide opportunities for success and mastery. The more accomplishments

they have, the better they feel about themselves. Come up with ways to make projects "friendly little competitions."

3. **Take a "one down" approach**. The old detective *Columbo*, played by Peter Faulk in the TV series, perfected this approach. Tell them you know they have vast knowledge and you would like to learn from them. Use a subtle submissive approach when asking them to do something. Rather than giving orders firmly, phrases like "I was wondering," "maybe," and "I know you are the expert, but what would you think if ..." may be more likely to be met with compliance and can be highly effective if they do not respond to a direct approach.

4. **Provide as much freedom and control as possible**. This doesn't mean you can't check in on them to make sure things are on track, but Bullies don't like to be closely monitored. Micromanage as little as possible. If you have some "control issue" yourself, you may need to check it a bit when dealing with this group. Put them in charge of task forces, work groups, and projects when appropriate. Bullies not only like to be in charge, but often have some traits that make them good leaders. Harness them when beneficial.

5. **Get good at setting and enforcing boundaries**. Draw a line in the sand when needed. Don't become aggressive and resist invitations to fight but hold your ground. Standing up for yourself in an assertive manner can actually help you command respect from the Bully. You can start small if you need to. And remember that even if they push you, you don't owe them an explanation. No is a complete sentence.

6. **Avoid power struggles**. Despite your best efforts to avoid potential arm-wrestling matches, if you are

regularly around a Bully chances are you will trigger them sooner or later. If they have, for whatever reason, identified you as a target of blame, they may come after you. As hard as it might be, remember arguing with a Bully, even if you are in the right, will only aggravate them and escalate the situation.

7. **Own your reality**. This is your best gaslighting repellent. Gaslighting only works when we give somebody else too much credit and don't give ourselves enough. Don't fall for their charisma or charm. I once heard it said that charisma is like heavy perfume someone wears when they didn't take a shower. If you encounter too much charisma, ask yourself what they are covering up. Just because they may be charming or articulate doesn't make them right.

8. **Don't take comments personally**. Of course, this is easier said than done. But all we can control is our reaction to them. But detach if possible. Monitor your thoughts. Remind yourself that this is how *they* are, that you aren't the only person they treat like this, and it means nothing about you! The better you get at this, the more power you will take back and the less they will trigger *you*.

9. **Limit interaction**. Sometimes, it is simply best to interact or encourage other employees to interact with Bullies as little as possible. Occasionally, this is the best course of action, even if only a temporary strategy. During required interactions, stick to business, accomplish your objective, and politely exit the conversation.

10. **Create a Bully-free work zone**. Sometimes a "three strikes and you're out" policy is necessary. Obviously you have company policies, local laws and industry regulations to abide by, but turning a blind eye,

transferring a complaining employee to a different department, or otherwise refusing to deal with the situation to hold the Bully accountable will only create further problems for your organization down the road. Leadership must set and adhere to some limits to maintain a work culture that good employees want to be a part of.

Speak their language

Now it is time to communicate strategically. Keeping in mind that communication involves a message sent plus a message received, and beliefs filter both ends of the interaction, what factors do you need to consider when preparing your BAM to deal with a Bully?

Remember our five questions from chapter 3?

1. Who am I?
2. Who are they?
3. Who are they to me?
4. Who am I to them?
5. How might I need to adapt my natural approach to speak their language?

What would using these as a template to prepare for a conversation actually look like?

Consider the following example: I once made the mistake of double-booking over a Skype meeting I had with an important Bully I had scheduled weeks in advance. Using the five question model outlined in chapter 3, my process looked a little bit like this:

1. Who am I?

Although I have a fair amount of *D* and *I* in my personality, my strongest trait is actually an *S*. The pure *S's* natural tendency would be to act in an extremely apologetic way and perhaps even agree to keep his appointment even though it was clearly not in my best interest based on priorities at the time.

2. Who are they?

I know from years of experience interacting with this individual that he is a Bully. He thinks extremely highly of himself and protecting his image is of the utmost importance. Ensuring the public maintains their high view of him and generating as much revenue as possible are always his top priorities. I've witnessed him verbally abuse several people over the years who made the unfortunate mistake of triggering him.

3. Who are they to me?

To me he is a highly reactive and punitive individual who easily angers. His conferences and training events also play an essential role in my speaking and training business. In addition to the *S* in me who wants to keep the peace, there are significant financial motivations that will affect the well-being of my family at stake here as well.

4. Who am I to them?

I am confident he respects my work. I know he at least likes me a decent amount on a personal level; however, I am also aware this will have a little bearing on his decisions regarding our working together moving forward. My workshops have drawn solid crowds and my evaluations have always been top-notch. If *those* factors remain unchanged, I will be in good shape to continue to work with him. However, when the quality of my content starts to diminish to the point that it affects my evaluations, I know I will no longer be an acceptable representation of his brand and image. When you are working with someone who sees themselves as superior to 99 percent of the competition there is little margin for error.

5. How do I need to adapt my natural approach to speak so they will listen?

Asking myself the question, "If my autopilot goes unchallenged, how would I likely send the message and how would he likely receive it?" my educated guess is that it might look like this:

My S "Autopilot" Filter	My Sending	His Filter	His Receiving
"Keep the peace"	"I am really sorry to have to do this. I can't believe I booked something over that we have scheduled. I have never done this before. I hope you will forgive me and there won't be any tension between us."	"I am special"	"Well that sounded a little grovelly. This is not how I want someone coming off in front of my large crowds. Maybe I should think twice about this guy."

I realize being as apologetic as my natural *S* tendencies would want me to may come across as "weak" to him. Since he only associates with other "special" people, I need to, in his mind's eye, keep myself in that 1 percent. He needs to hear that I am sorry for inconveniencing him and that my number one motive is to deliver in a way that builds his brand and protects his image.

Now that you have received a scary look into my thought processes, let's see what that looks like in the form of a BAM.

Example BAM

B "Hey, Mike—I hate to do this—I know your time is valuable, but I am going to have to move our appointment."

A "I could still do it, but would have to cut it short, and I want to devote the time it needs for me to continue to deliver the great content that draws the crowds we are used to and keep this event elite."

M "You name a time that works for you any time in the next two weeks and I will do what it takes to accommodate my schedule."

What did you notice about this BAM response? Did I offer extensive explanations involving details? Did I gush on in apologetic language? Did I even mention relationships or feelings? The answer to all of these is no. It is brief (which all **D's** prefer), and it speaks to his high opinion of his company, the worth of his time, and the autonomy to control when we reschedule.

Setting boundaries and enforcing consequences

In the above example, my specific goal for the interaction was to avoid an attack, and ultimately not damage a business relationship by disarming the bomb before the fuse ever got lit. Remember, one of the general strategies will always be to know what triggers that particular type of HC person and do what you can to avoid engaging in behaviors or using words prone to set them off. By accomplishing this, I was never attacked and there was no need for boundary setting. However, if my attempt to disarm would have been unsuccessful, I may have needed to move to this stage.

To further illustrate this, remember Sara from chapter 3? Her initial goal was to end the abusive language on that particular phone call. You may recall I mentioned that she eventually ended the abusive relationship, but only after a series of interactions that required setting and enforcing boundaries. For example, one of her interactions went like this:

B "Joe, you are incredibly gifted at what you do. You are the best in the industry. People worship you for it. You have bought me nice things and allowed me to share in some pretty cool experiences I would never in a million years have had the opportunity to experience without you."

A "I think deep down you have a good heart, but there have been several times when you have lost your temper like you did yesterday that I have gotten injured. Last night was the first time Sadie got hurt. I think you know my daughter is the most important thing in the world to me and I will do whatever it takes to keep her safe."

M "There is part of me that doesn't want to do this ... and I don't think deep down in you want me to do this. But I need you to know, that if you get physical ever again, with her or with me, I'm done."

Recall the guidelines for setting boundaries from chapter 3.

1. Was Sara clear about the boundary? Yes. "If you ever get physical with me again" is a pretty clear

boundary that can be measured and quantified. Her previous language "treat me with respect" was too vague and up for interpretation. But this line was clear—touching her or her daughter physically in any way out of anger again was unacceptable.

2. Was Sara clear about the consequences? Yes. She said, "we are done," meaning the relationship would end.

3. Did Sara enforce the consequences? Although you can't see this from this interaction, the answer is … not immediately, but eventually. The first time she gave in and said she "didn't know if she could follow through." So we made a list of potential consequences she believed she could enforce. The next time she slept in a separate bedroom for a week. When it then happened again, she left the house entirely for the weekend. The next time it happened she moved in with her mom for a week. Her next step was to get a six-month lease on an apartment of her own. It should be noted that Joe's behavior in fact did change significantly, and they had several positive dating interactions while no longer living together. But as Sara continued to grow, despite his best efforts and some authentic change, she realized considering her new life goals, the two of them were just not the best fit.

Know when to walk away, know when to run

The line from the Kenny Rogers song "The Gambler" offers solid advice when dealing with any HC personality. While some people err on the side of removing themselves too soon when a Bully is around, others suffer for extended periods of time due to being unwilling to walk away. I have had clients quit jobs due to one interaction with an HC person. They cost themselves tremendous career opportunities by refusing even to try to deal with the difficult person strategically. Many others have damaged themselves or others they care about enormously by refusing to break up with, fire, expel, or otherwise leave a difficult person. Sometimes making the tough call to terminate an employee, have a student removed from a classroom, walk away from a job, or leave an abusive significant other is the most freeing decision you will ever make—and it's a decision that often benefits people you care about as well. There is always a time to say enough is enough. But knowing when that time is can be difficult to determine. Each chapter in this section will conclude with a few paragraphs addressing this issue with each particular type of HC person.

In terms of dealing with a Bully, Sara's final step of enforcement involved breaking the relationship off completely and she has had no contact with him since. Although this was an extremely difficult process, she eventually realized she would be better off without him. Sara's story serves as a powerful testimony that we as people can come to believe ideas we once did not, and these mindset changes can, indeed, allow us to get out of situations we at one point did not believe were possible.

This BAM and subsequent follow-through differs a little from most examples. Although she initially couldn't articulate it in this way, Sara knew at some level she was important to his sense of feeling special. Although he appeared on the surface to "have it all together," the reality was that the only elements feeding Joe's identity were his occupation and his relationship with Sara. Her physical attractiveness, charismatic personality, and quick wit highlighted the qualities that made Joe the object of much jealousy in his industry that was on showcase at their regular events. Her putting the relationship on the line—and taking steps to show she meant it, threatened the very nature of what made him special. This use of leverage stopped him in his tracks, and disarmed a Bully in ways that no outside observer imagined was possible.

We all, like Sara, have to weigh carefully the pros and cons of maintaining the status quo in our relationships with Bullies we come across in our lives. After thoughtful consideration, if and when you decide the consequences of staying in the relationship have already been or will likely be more damaging than you will tolerate, you know it's time to walk away—and sometimes run. Sadly, this is often required with Bullies.

5

The Con Artist

"They have no regard for the social contract,
but they do know how to use it to their advantage."

—Martha Stout, The Sociopath Next Door

Beliefs: "I must serve own interests only; others don't matter."

Behaviors: Verbal aggression, lying, threats, deceiving, tricking others with no remorse

Mindset: "Get what I want no matter what it takes"

DISC parallel: One out of control manifestation of the *D*

Clinical parallel: One out of control manifestation of the *D*.

Continuum

Mild	Moderate	Severe
I----------------------I----------------------I		
Likable on the surface	Occasional lies,	Blatant disregard
Level, but can't	threats, or	for rules, procedures,
trust them	May even hurt	chain of command
To be telling	others	Just doing what
the truth	or break laws	they want to
		Seen as "rebellious"

Description

T he Con Artist represents a different type of out of control version of the *D* prototype on the DISC profile, and in clinical terms, often has traits of *antisocial* personality traits. As with all trait sets addressed in this book, the Con Artist comes in many different "flavors," many of which are not diagnosable.

Con Artists are generally charming, direct, and will do *anything* to get what they want. They have an "anti-society"/counterculture mindset that drives behaviors that violate rules, laws, societal norms, and at times other people. They can act impulsively, but also have the capacity to commit premeditated acts in very calculating ways.

When I present this material at live events, I often get asked versions of "I thought the Bully was the out of control version of the *D*; how can the Con Artist be also?" Keep in mind that each primary DISC style can have multiple "out of control" manifestations. It may be helpful to remember that the Con Artist is primarily interested in being *rebellious*, while the Bully is more interested in being perceived as *special*. Both might run over people en route to their respective goals; however, underlying motives are usually significantly different.

In terms of the DISC, Con Artists do qualify as ***D's*** because they are task oriented, in the sense that they always focus on getting what they want, and they are outgoing in the sense that they often have a high "motor."

Many novice people-handlers believe Con Artists are people oriented because they are typically very charming, and it would appear on the surface that they enjoy people. Consider the many politicians running for office that often have a very "smooth" communication style. They elicit approval from others, and they may, to some extent, enjoy people, but ultimately people are only a means to an end. The Con Artist sees people as simply objects to be used to get what they want and they use charm as one of their strategies to get it.

Because Con Artists have the gift of charming others and the charisma mentioned above, they also often propel themselves to leadership positions. A perhaps unnoticed characteristic of the Con Artist is that they typically have lower anxiety levels than the rest of us. This quality enables them to take charge easily, withstand criticism and outside pressure without getting rattled, make decisions with very little hesitation, and project the image organizations often look for in new candidates. In contrast to the Bully who often puts on a front of confidence to mask inferiority at their core, Con Artists usually legitimately believe in their abilities and ultimate superiority.

On the downside, their willingness to do whatever it takes to get what they want often drives them to break rules and sometimes laws that get themselves or the organizations they work for in trouble. There may also be times the Con Artist's desires conflict with the best interests of the organization they work for. In instances that they get caught in one of their lies, it can significantly damage the credibility of their employer.

Fewer extreme versions of the Con Artist likely show up in the everyday lives of most of you reading this book. Unfortunately, many of these people are in prison. However, as Martha Stout points out in her *The New York Times* best seller *The Sociopath Next Door*, "Con Artists could be your neighbor and you likely wouldn't even know it! I mean, what does the guy reporters always interview on TV always say about the mass murderer or person who set off the bomb? *'He was such a quiet person.'* Or *'She was the last person I would have expected to do something like this.'*"

The reality is that most people these days are relatively unobservant, lack awareness, or love to give people the benefit of the doubt, so perhaps we should not expect them to "expect it." However, Con Artists are often strategically controlled and can be quite calculating, enabling them to be scheming something for an extended period of time while legitimately showing no outward signs to the casual observer.

It is surprising to many that in addition to being prevalent in gangs, drug cartels, and prisons (places people expect them to be), as Robert Hare points out in his book *Snakes in Suits: When Psychopaths Go to Work*, Con Artists are also more common than most would ever believe in the upper echelons of our society as well.

Many ambulance chasing attorneys make millions of dollars lying, deceiving, and fabricating the truth for a living. While we see the occasional corporate scandal where guilty parties actually do suffer consequences (Bernie Madoff), traits that drive Con Artists also can enable executives to take advantage of employees, stakeholders, or other affected parties in horribly callous and unemotional ways without technically even breaking the law. As an avid sports fan, I also have to acknowledge that some of the teams I follow enable a culture that has allowed lawbreaking behaviors to go unpunished regularly. While the Aaron Hernandez case represents extreme exceptions, this culture unfortunately is all too common in professional, and perhaps to a lesser degree, college athletics. These are only a few areas Con Artists show up in everyday life.

Con Artists believe that rules, norms, and laws, as well as other people are irrelevant. Common attitudes produced by this belief set include:

- ♣ "It's OK to lie, because it is necessary to get what I want."
- ♣ "If I have to hurt her, I will. She should have stayed out of my way."
- ♣ "This rule is BS anyway—I will just do what I want."
- ♣ "He deserved it—he shouldn't have tried to stop me."

Red flags

As with traits of every personality style, you can always spot Con Artists ahead of time if you know what to look for. Here are a few red flags to keep an eye out for in different settings.

Red flags for Con Artists in the workplace

- ☐ Do they have a history of rule-breaking complaints or terminations in previous employment?
- ☐ Were there any red flags AT ALL on the criminal background check?
- ☐ Do references report any history of lying, aggression or rule/policy breaking on the job?
- ☐ If there were complaints, when you ask about them, what do they say? Do you notice blaming others, discounting rules or policies, or minimizing?
- ☐ Do they take any responsibility for the problematic behaviors?
- ☐ Describe a scenario in your unit or department where a typical employee might feel tempted to skirt the rules. Note their response carefully.
- ☐ Describe a scenario where an employee was taken advantage of and ask how they would respond to it. Observe closely for remorse, sympathy, and compassion

Red flags for Con Artists in educational settings

- ☐ Do they have a history of cruelty to animals?
- ☐ Do they have a history of bed-wetting?
- ☐ Do they have a history of fire starting?
- ☐ Did they get in trouble in earlier grades, dating back to Pre-K?
- ☐ Do they have a history of not following the rules at church, scouts, sports, or other extracurricular activities?
- ☐ Do they have a history of bullying?
- ☐ Do you observe bullying in the classroom or on the playground?

☐ If they break a rule or get in an altercation, do they appear remorseful for it after they have calmed down?

☐ Do they socialize with peers? If so, what types of friends do they hang out with?

Red flags for Con Artists in faith-based settings

☐ Do they name-call, use demeaning terms, etc., even if in a "joking" way? How do they treat the other people in their life?

☐ Do you hear them bragging about "sham jobs" or how they "pulled one over" on someone?

☐ Are you typically attracted to the "bad boy" (or girl)?

☐ Do they do things considered counterculture / against the norms of society?

☐ Do you observe them breaking rules or laws?

☐ Are you drawn in by their charisma, bravery, or thrill-seeking acts?

☐ Do they struggle with anger?

☐ Do they see it as their job to put somebody in their place?

☐ Do they think it's funny when others are legitimately hurting?

☐ Intense eye contact

A relationship example

Tonya was a thirty-eight-year-old woman with a petite figure and a raspy voice who showed up for her first appointment with me wearing leather pants and boots. She said she needed help because she was "a little sad."

Upon evaluation, I observed that Tania was more than just a little sad. She was diagnosed clinically depressed and likely had a full-blown eating disorder as well.

Tonya had no job, no friends, and had difficulty verbalizing hobbies or anything she did for fun. She had a "hot and cold relationship with her mother," and only one other lady from a support group who she kept up with.

The area of her life she was most eager to talk about was the new man in her life, Joe. When I asked what Joe did for a living, she responded by saying, "He runs his own business."

When I asked what line of work he was in she responded by saying, "I'm not really sure."

When I asked her what she liked about Joe she said, "He makes me feel safe."

Tonya also revealed that she had "a thing for tattoos and muscles" and Joe definitely fit the bill.

Further exploration revealed that the first night they hung out together he bragged about being kicked out of school, winning multiple bar fights, and being able to "hook her up" if she needed a "pick me up" or "a little relaxation." He also smirked as he alluded to having been known to "spend a night or two in jail."

Unlike previous boyfriends Tania had been with that liked to talk big, but didn't have much "bite behind their bark", on their second date she actually witnessed him hurt a person with a knife who attempted to slip in the door to his cocaine dealers ahead of him. Tonya said, "I felt terrible and told him we should not leave the guy there bleeding, but he told me, 'He should not have tried to go in the door ahead of me. He should know I don't need an appointment.'"

When I asked Tonya if Joe had ever harmed her physically, she said, "only once or twice. He is usually a real gentleman. And you should see the respect he has for his mother. I was so impressed."

When I asked Tonya if she had any idea what might be contributing to her "sadness," she said she wasn't sure. I suggested that perhaps she could think about it for homework and we could discuss it at the next session. She agreed, and eagerly said, "Can Joe come in with me to the next session? He is really smart. He would probably like psychotherapy."

A school example

Curtis was his fourth-grade teacher, Miss Grigsby's biggest nightmare. At twenty-three years old, she was fresh out of school and just coming off her final student teaching semester. She was intelligent, highly motivated, and excited to have her first class of her own. That was until the first day when she met Curtis. He never followed directions and rarely did his schoolwork. When confronted by the teacher he was blatantly defiant. The other kids thought it was funny when he put her down in front of the rest of the class. She told him he would get bad grades. He did not seem to care. She threatened to take away his recess. Again, he did not seem to care. She offered to reward him for good behavior and work habits. He definitely did not care. She finally decided to call his parents to request a meeting to discuss his behavior. Miss Grigsby discovered his father did not live in the home and his mother was not only not interested in making an appointment, but she accused her of treating her son poorly. She said she was "not doing her job and teaching him anything."

Exasperated and with all her enthusiasm zapped, she finally contacted the associate principal in charge of discipline to ask what they could do. All the ideas she had for dealing with him got rejected. She was told any punitive action was unacceptable, but they were willing to test him to see if they could put him on an individualized education plan. Although he did qualify for some special services, his mother refused, stating "he will feel like even more of an outcast. You all just need to learn how to do your job." The rest of the school year, Curtis punched three other students, bragged to his peers about torturing his cat at home, and was visited by the police at school one day for being accused of setting a fire in a local business. Although they held IEP meetings regularly, Miss Grigsby was prohibited from any disciplinary action and Curtis's behavior worsened throughout the school year. Ms. Grigsby resigned on the last day of school and has not returned to teaching since.

Connecting with the Con Artist

Connecting is a foundational element of communicating effectively with anyone. And this truth is only amplified when dealing with difficult people. Unfortunately, Con Artists really don't truly connect with much of anybody. Much of the time, the best you can hope for is to earn their "respect."

Here are a few tips:

- ❖ **Shoot straight**. Like the Bully, this type is not much for excessive talk. Get to the point. Don't try to sugar coat, beat around the bush, or reframe. Be direct and tell it like it is.
- ❖ **Take an interest in their sham jobs**. Some people criticize me for suggesting this one. But let me be clear—it is possible to convey an interest in what they are up to without condoning the behavior. Being interested in their life including behavior that would not pass your moral compass is necessary if you hope to open a door to get through to them.

❖ **If you have any "rebel" in you, let them see it.** This can be minor. It may not include lawbreaking behaviors. Any sense of "anti-authority" or "antiestablishment" you may have, even if contained, will be respected by this type. If you authentically don't have this in you, be yourself. Con Artists know immediately if you are faking. You will gain more respect by just being you.

❖ **Validate the grain of truth** before making a request or statement. Even if you know their intent or disagree with them 99 percent of the time, find *something* they say, even if it is the smallest "grain" in the entire conversation, and validate it. For example, you can start with: *"Yes, I agree there are a lot of idiots in the world who can easily be taken advantage of … and"* … say what you want to tell them. This (1) connects with them when you show you have at least a small point of agreement, and (2) disarms them by not activating their defenses before you even get to make your request.

Top ten tips for disarming the Con Artist

1. **Know their triggers and avoid them.** Con Artists get triggered by laws, rules, norms, or anything that threatens their sense of autonomy or desires. They believe they can do whatever they please to get what they want. Since many true psychopaths end up in prison, and those who don't typically aren't pursuing an education, seeking traditional employment, or attending church services, most readers of this book are likely not surrounded by extreme versions of this style. However, we all have "rebels" in our worlds. Armed with the knowledge that this

personality type has the mentality of a Con Artist can inform our people-handing when dealing with them. Don't push unnecessary rules. Instead, find out their motivations and give them options to get what they want within the confines of the rules.

2. **Find ways to harness their low anxiety.** There are many contexts it serves a person well to have low anxiety levels in the face of pressure. This quality serves individuals well in law enforcement, fire-fighters, active-duty military and even politicians. Although many job descriptions don't require this degree of actual danger, you can harness this quality in smaller practical ways. Eighth-grade basketball coaches use this technique when designing plays for who they want to take the game-winning shot. The coach usually chooses someone who has "ice in their veins," and is cool under pressure rather than the teammate who can only hit ten out of ten in practice. This "antiestablishment" mentality, if kept in check, can benefit many other roles, including advocacy roles, human resources, and attorneys.

3. **Separate them when possible.** This technique min-imizes their ability to stir up controversy or create problems. Let them work remotely when possible. Separate them in classrooms. Strategically con-sider what office to assign them to. Separation can sometimes disarm the bomb before it goes off. Put distancing safeguards in place. This is a person you probably never want to assign to be alone with a peer or coworker. A cloud of witnesses is always the best policy when dealing with Con Artists. If the person has a history of physical violence, refrain from having any conversations that even entail dis-agreements with them alone in your classroom or

office. When red flags arise, it can be wise to require that any discussion around a problem issue or with a problem person be via email, thereby creating a paper trail of what is actually said.

4. **Fact check.** *"Trust but verify"* became a well-known phrase associated with president Ronald Regan within the context of nuclear talks during the cold war with the USSR in the 1980s. While we never want to assume anyone is lying, Con Artists are notoriously untrustworthy, and their work often needs verification. Cheating on exams, fabricating hours, and manipulating others with no remorse or repentance is commonplace with this personality style. If there is any doubt, verify to ensure you have the facts straight before moving forward with a plan of action. So, before confronting the situation, you may need to collect evidence to prevent manipulation of the facts.

5. **Confront lies.** Allowing lies to go unchallenged encourages the person to continue to lie. Instead, when time and setting are appropriate, let them know you know what they are up to give them a chance to be honest with you by asking for the truth.

6. **Identify the function of the lie.** Lying is never OK, but how you respond may differ depending on the reason behind the behavior. For example, the employee stealing coworkers' food from the lounge refrigerator because she doesn't have enough food for her children may be dealt with differently than the partner who continually cheats or the person who embezzles company funds for personal profit.

7. **Leverage consequences.** Research has shown that *meaningful consequences* can be as effective any just about anything, including years of therapy, to get

Con Artists to modify their behavior. This is never the most pleasant approach, but if you have to hold something over someone's head to elicit the behavior you want, the situation isn't good in the first place. You don't want to threaten them, but remember to frame consequences in terms of not getting what they want. Never make idle threats. Reminders that "I need you to stay clean for me and our daughter to stay in this house, and that's what I want most" or "we really need you on this team, so I am sure hoping you are filling out your reports honestly" can go a long way.

8. **No wiggle room**. Many of us like to give people the benefit of the doubt. With this group, we just cannot give the benefit of the doubt. If you are a people person you like to see the good in others. While this is an admirable trait and serves us well sometimes, it also can disable our radar to pick up on harm that may be present. Remember, this group is inherently dishonest. Tricking people is their primary strategy, and the reality is if they are better at conning than we are at recognizing it, we will do nobody any good at all. With this type, we must stick with the consequences we set.

9. **Collaborate to minimize deception**. One great way to disarm manipulation is to communicate clearly with all others involved. For example, if three different teachers supervised the Con Artist during music, recess, and speech therapy, go out of your way to talk with each of them so you will know what the truth is when the student returns to your classroom. Likewise, insist the corporate coach speak with the Con Artist's direct supervisor, his wife, and one coworker before each session. Collaboration

ensures you have the correct information to prepare for dealing with them effectively.

10. **Bring in a third party**. There are times there is no other option. This style is as resistant to change as any HC type. Going to management, having a family meeting, or hiring a mediator is sometimes a necessary step.

Speak their language

Now it is time to communicate strategically. Keeping in mind that communication involves a message sent plus a message received, and that beliefs filter both ends of the interaction, what factors might be important to consider when preparing your BAM to deal with a Con Artist?

Remember our five questions?

1. Who am I?
2. Who are they?
3. Who are they to me?
4. Who am I to them?
5. How do I need to adapt my natural approach to speak so they will listen?

Disarming a Con Artist is a little bit different than disarming the other types of HC personalities. They are different because Con Artists have a different belief system than just about everybody else. Because of this it is a lot more difficult to "stop them in their tracks" than it is to get to them to begrudgingly do what it is that you want them to do. But, sometimes with the most difficult of people, you take what you can get.

The most effective strategies for dealing with this type of HC person include:

♣ Involving somebody they actually do care about
♣ Making it very difficult for them to get what they want by continuing to break the rules.

William was an inmate I once met within a medium-security penitentiary. He was being asked to change a specific behavior in the cafeteria by the correctional staff. Actually, they ordered him to do so. However, since Con Artists don't do well when told what to do, his behavior only escalated.

So keeping our five questions in mind, what would using these as a template to prepare for a conversation with Will actually look like?

1. Who am I?

Although I have a fair amount of *D* and *I* in my personality, my strongest trait is an *S*. The Pure *S's* natural tendency would want to approach this in a very timid manner and perhaps not even have the conversation at all. But I did want better for him than he was going to get if his behavior remained unchanged.

2. Who are they?

I know from speaking with correctional officials and listening to some of the things he has said to me (not to mention the behaviors he was incarcerated for) that he can be a Con Artist. He has a disregard for the rules, does not like to be told what to do, and is triggered just about any time he gets challenged or "dissed."

3. Who are they to me?

To me he is a dangerous person who easily angers. Although I know what my motives for him truly are, and part of me knows that with the rapport I have built with him he likely wouldn't hurt me, the **S** in me is still hesitant to confront the issue.

4. Who am I to them?

I think he appreciates what I am doing to help him. He probably still views me as a bit of a naive "softy," but I think he knows I have his back. Based on my perception of his accurate appraisal of my intent, I will move forward.

5. How might I need to adapt my natural approach to speak so they will listen?

Asking myself the question, "If my autopilot mindset goes unchallenged, how would I likely send the message and how would he likely receive it?" my educated guess is that it might look like this:

My S "Autopilot" Filter	My Sending	His Filter	His Receiving
"Keep the peace"	Possibility 1: Not say anything to him Possibility 2: Don't you think you should not keep making him mad like that?	"Do anything to get what you want"	"Jeff means well, but be damned if I'm going to keep letting this officer be a jerk."

Knowing he was up for parole soon, and he was not likely going to change his behavior regardless, I decided I needed to say something, mention his daughter, and send my message a little more directly than my natural tendencies might dictate. My initial BAM looked like this:

B "Will—I know you are pretty much used to getting what you want and I know you are not about to let some correctional officer like Delbert show you up in a disrespectful way in front of everyone in the cafeteria."

A "I also know your daughter means the world to you and I think you know she needs her father in her life right now—I'm only saying this because I want what's best for you ... and her."

M "So I really hope you will remind yourself that if you continue to let some lowlife in the cafeteria get the best of you, you are giving him more importance in your life and Ashlee. You've got to decide. Is it more important for you to save face in front of the guys and piss him off? Or for Ashlee to get her dad back again soon?"

What did you notice about my communication? Did I hesitate, stammer, or apologize for possibly stepping on his toes? You could not evaluate my tone of voice, but I did not. I was direct, communicated my intent, made a suggestion, and left the ball in his court (control over the decision).

Setting boundaries and enforcing consequences

When I confronted Will, he went completely silent for the first time I had ever seen. I concluded with my final.

"If you exercise more self-control than him and stop what you're doing in the cafeteria starting tomorrow, my guess is you will have a lot better odds when the parole board meets the next month."

If you recall our guidelines for setting boundaries in chapter 3, you will recognize exactly what I am doing here.

1. Was I clear about the boundary? Yes. Because I can tell by his non-verbal cues, I actually have him thinking here, and I follow up immediately with a request for changed behavior. We both knew what "changing the cafeteria behavior" meant. Brief is best with Con Artists.

2. Was I clear about the consequences? Fairly. Because consequences can feel like a threat to a Con Artist (and you may recall this is one sure way to trigger them), I am framing this statement to him using alternate verbiage to speak his language. That is, rather than just come right out and directly state the likely consequences of him not changing his behavior, I list the likely reward of him choosing to change his behavior, and, by doing so, only imply the consequence as part of the flip side of the coin. My goal is to point this out and quickly put the ball back in his court.

3. Was there follow-through? This situation is slightly different in that I don't personally administer consequences—I am just pointing out to him the likely natural consequences if he fails to change his behavior.

Know when to walk away, know when to run

Sometimes Con Artists can be enticed to change their behavior. Still, there comes a point when violating behaviors become too much for a relationship, organization, or any other entity to stand. In determining when to cut their losses, one must weigh the long-term benefits for the Con

Artist and the other people/organizations that may be involved. Once you consider all factors and receive input from the appropriate people, if the anti-authoritarian behaviors do more harm than good, it may be in the best interest of everybody for the Con Artist to be terminated, expelled from school, or otherwise removed. Rule and agreement-breaking behaviors are often the most difficult for personal relationships, academic environments, and work cultures to withstand. Possibly more often with this group than any other HC type, cutting losses and moving on is in the best interest of all involved.

6

The Drama Mamma

"No one ever told me I was pretty. All girls should be told they are pretty, even if they aren't."

—Marilyn Monroe

Beliefs: "I am noteworthy" "The world is a playground!"

Mindset: "Life was meant to be a party. Make it one!"

Behaviors: Spontaneous behaviors, dramatic displays of emotion, attention-seeking

DISC parallel: One out of control manifestation of the *I*

Clinical parallel: A person with *histrionic personality* traits.

Continuum

Mild	Moderate	Severe
I-------------------------I-------------------------I		
Demonstrative, Vivid expressions Mild exaggeration but can be redirected	Mild attention-seeking Extreme language Stirs up "drama" environments – not	Need to be center of Attention is disruptive to relationships or work easily redirected

Description

The Drama Mamma (DM) represents an out of control version of the *I* prototype on the DISC personality profile, and in clinical terms has *histrionic* personality traits. However, it is important to note that many people have some narcissistic traits who are not fully diagnosable with histrionic personality disorder.

When kept in check, this type of person can be a lot of fun. They can be the life of the party and help others enjoy themselves. They are inspiring, spontaneous, and energetic. They can help make even the most mundane of projects or requirements seem fun.

On the downside, there are situations in life that require seriousness. The Drama Mamma (DM) is prone to lose focus and miss deadlines. When they insert unnecessary or inappropriate drama into serious situations, it can pose a risk to required accomplishments and even compromise safety at times. Their need to be the center of attention is not always harmless given the situation.

DMs often come across as fun, confident, and vivacious. Because of this outward presentation, many people believe they have healthy self-esteem. I have had young ladies say to me things like "I wish I had her confidence. She just goes up to a guy and starts talking and isn't even nervous. I don't know how she does that!" The reality is, however, that deep down, DMs are quite insecure as well. Getting a laugh at the party, a "double-take" from a guy, or a round of applause from a crowd are necessary boosts to a well-disguised low self-esteem. Zig Ziglar is famous for saying "Motivation doesn't last—and neither does bathing, that's why we recommend both daily!"

It is a little like this for the DM. Eliciting these responses (usually) from the opposite sex makes them the center of attention and creates a temporary "high," but the warm fuzzy feelings don't last. Thus, they feel the need to continue behaving in their theatrical ways day after day. While the responses to these actions continue to stroke the ego of the DM, they often wear others out.

While extreme language has become an epidemic in our society, this group takes the cake when it comes to hyperbole. Expressions such as *"the best," "the worst,"* and *"the end of the world!"* characterize the everyday language of the DM. You may also observe them being overly concerned with appearance, body image, and the like, making comments about their weight (*"I gained two pounds this week"*) or clothing (*"This isn't normally the style I look best in, but I was in Saks Fifth Avenue yesterday so I thought what the heck."*) Friendly, lighthearted, joking, flirtatious, and sometimes even sexually seductive behavior is commonly seen in people with these traits. In school settings, various types of "class clown" behavior disrupt classrooms.

While most of us prefer to have as little drama in our lives as possible, some people thrive on it. Some of these attempts to gain favor or attention in the eyes of others are less draining than others, and some can even be helpful in the right setting and for shorter periods. But too much drama is draining for everyone and ultimately wears out even the DM herself. I once heard that "drama is only funny if it is in third person or past tense."

As with each of these types, traits manifest on a continuum. People who fall in the mild to moderate category may annoy fewer people in life and as pointed out, can be quite funny. More extreme versions of DMs not only enjoy being "on stage," but feel like they NEED to be in the spotlight and feel slighted if and when they are not. These individuals with more "out of control" traits often engage in more extreme behaviors to get your attention. Acting out behaviors might include loud emotional outbursts, pouting, onset of sudden illness, tearfulness, or even sexually inappropriate innuendo.

Due to needing ongoing and seemingly constant validation from others, you might have guessed DMs are also easily influenced by those around them. "Moodiness" and the more extreme behaviors described above are always responses to lack of such validation.

Some examples of DM attitudes can be seen in the following statements:

- ♣ "If I get noticed, I have value."
- ♣ "If I tell a big story, I will get attention."
- ♣ "If I stretch the truth, people will think I am funnier."
- ♣ "If I am funny, kids in the class will like me."
- ♣ "Being physically attractive gets me noticed."
- ♣ "Having a hot partner means I have value."
- ♣ "If I act up, I will get my teacher's attention."
- ♣ "If I can make others laugh, they will notice me."
- ♣ "If I am sick, I will be the focus of others' attention."

Remember everything we do, we do for a reason. And everything we do repeatedly we do because it "works." That is, we get something out of it. In some cases, the cons or potential cons significantly outweigh the pros, but the benefit must be worth it to continue to make the same choices. Some people are unaware of the consequences of certain behaviors and can benefit from having them pointed out in a caring way. Others know the consequences of a given behavior, but the short-term satisfaction makes it worth it.

Many DMs don't realize the harm their choices cause themselves or others. There is nothing wrong with being attractive and gaining some sense of value and satisfaction from that. But when those qualities become the *only* source of worth somebody sees in themselves, the more desperately they will go out of their way to seek that kind of reinforcement, since positive feedback in other areas doesn't seem to matter.

Many reading this may be familiar with the epic civil war drama *Gone with the Wind*. The 1939 film was adapted from Margaret Mitchell's novel just three years prior, and starred Vivien Leigh as Scarlett O'Hara. While I was vaguely familiar with the movie due to its classic status, it wasn't until I lectured in Atlanta one time that my eyes were truly opened. Leaving the suburb of Marietta after presenting, I drove past the Gone with the Wind Museum, and couldn't help stopping and swinging in for a glance at what the displays had to offer. Although I did see some pretty interesting stuff (if you are into Southern US history), I also encountered some information that struck me as a little disturbing. I discovered that Leigh really wasn't acting much when she played Scarlett. Though she was known as one of the most physically attractive actresses Hollywood has ever seen, her beauty in some ways became the bane of her existence. Her life was one of much instability including multiple marriages/partners, numerous breakdowns on and off stage, multiple affairs, substance use, and even suicide threats and attempts as her beauty, from her perspective, faded as she entered her forties. Although her ultimate cause of death was officially considered tuberculous, the actress became known for physical beauty masking emotional torment.

Red flags

As with traits of each personality style, you can spot DMs ahead of time if you know what to look for. Here are a few red flags to keep an eye out for in different settings.

Drama Mamma red flags in the workplace

- ☐ Are they demonstrative or overly talkative in their interview?
- ☐ Is there anything "over the top" with how they dress (note shoes, hats, accessories, etc.)
- ☐ Listen for how they characterize previous workplace interactions. What qualities do they value in coworkers?
- ☐ Do they tell "fish stories"? Listen for exaggeration or blowing things out of proportion.
- ☐ Ask them about the longest project they worked on or were responsible for. Purposefully tune into their tendency to stick something through in the long run versus getting easily distracted or quitting.

- ☐ Do you observe (or has there been reported) overly flirtatious behavior in the workplace?
- ☐ Ask them a serious question. Gauge their ability to engage a relevant subject matter at a deeper level.

Drama Mamma red flags in schools

- ☐ Do they show tendencies to be the "class clown?"
- ☐ Do they use humor to bring attention to themselves?
- ☐ Do they always seem to have to "one-up" someone else's story or performance?
- ☐ Pay attention to their ability to be alone.
- ☐ Do they throw temper tantrums, yell, scream, or otherwise act out when not the center of attention?
- ☐ Do they appear sad or forlorn when not gaining sufficient attention?
- ☐ Do they spend significant time in the nurse's office with no apparent medical problems?

Drama Mamma red flags in personal relationships

- ☐ Do they act like you are closer than you perceive the relationship to be?
- ☐ What is their history of friendships like? Do they have long-lasting, deeply connected relationships? Or do they always seem to have a new partner or circle of friends with each season of life?
- ☐ Does everything seem to be a big deal? Do they blow things out of proportion?
- ☐ Are they prone to gossip? Do they always seem to have to be "breaking news" about others?
- ☐ What is their history of dating and romantic relationships like? Have they dated people for sustained

periods? Or do they have a pattern of short-lived relationships?

☐ Do they often joke about members of the opposite sex being "hot" or make frequent references to physical appearance, even if "joking?"

Purposefully listen for their ability to have an empathetic conversation about someone else. Do they get bored? Quickly shift the topic or relate it in some way to themselves?

A school example

Maci Grew up hearing she was the most beautiful girl in the world. While this might sound like a nice message on the surface, her parents took this to a whole different level. Her father was the quarterback on his high school football team, and her mother was the homecoming queen. They viewed themselves as the perfect "power couple." Prior to her conception, her mother fantasized about having "the perfect little girl." Her parents enrolled her in her first beauty pageant at age six. Maci had average intelligence and worked hard to make good grades. She enjoyed tennis and was a naturally gifted pianist. However, despite her tennis tournament victories, her straight-A report card, and her invitation to the gifted music program in middle school, the only positive strokes she got from her parents growing up were concerning her pageant successes. "Nothing matters nearly as much as how a person looks" was the message she continued to receive from her parents. The day they purchased her first bra was more celebrated than her eighth-grade graduation, and while there was no money for tennis camp, she had an unlimited budget for mascara.

By her freshman in high school, Maci only played tennis occasionally, had given up the piano completely, and barely passed most of her classes. She was involved in thespians and had a long string of "on and off" boyfriends. Mother "jokingly" commented regularly about how "hot" her boyfriends were. She spent a lot of time in the school nurse's office when she was supposed to be in class. Even at age fifteen, she could say "I learned early in life what it takes in this world: you have to have a little flair and you have to know how to get the right people's attention."

A church example

"Shelly" was a therapist by trade, though many members of her church community wondered how. She always showed up to functions dressed to the nines, and she was never seen in public without a generous amount of mascara and a pair of high heels. While she rarely dated among her singles group, when she did it was always the men who had the best jobs and the most distinguished houses.

On the surface she was likable enough. Her charisma did have a way of lighting up a room, and her laughter was contagious. She was the life of every party, and in small doses, made get-togethers much more entertaining. Shelly was always "breaking news" of some kind and a function wasn't complete without one of her big announcements that usually started with "You all are not going to believe this!" ... She really could be a lot of fun! People also occasionally got annoyed with her theatrics, however, and her gossip was sometimes quite hurtful.

One evening at Bible study, she delivered the proverbial straw that broke the camel's back. Stacie, one of the shyest members of the group who rarely shared prayer requests, verbalized, with a quiver in her voice and a tear in her eye, the week of her fortieth birthday she had been diagnosed with cancer and it had already spread significantly before it was detected. The group was stunned, and nobody quite knew what to say. Awkwardly, people broke the silence by offering to pray for her, support her, and ask her how they could help. Several offers were given, hugs were exchanged, and tears were shed. To combat the heaviness of the mood in the room, Ronnie offered to close the group in prayer. Before he could, however, Shelly verbalized a request to be prayed for as well. Although her request was "unspoken" it vaguely pertained to a situation involving her niece having her feelings hurt over an incident at the school prom. She then flung herself off the couch and broke out into a song performed earlier in the week on television by the latest outcast of *American Idol*.

Shelly's need to be the center of attention could not even be curbed by the seriousness of a moment such as a member of her own church family being diagnosed with a possible terminal condition. Her outburst displayed a level of insensitivity few realized even she was capable of. Spontaneity can be exciting and we generally like engaging people. But the insensitivity Shelly showed that night out of her need to be the center of attention will never be forgotten by people in that room.

Connecting with the Drama Mamma

Connecting is a foundational element of communicating effectively with anyone. And this truth is only amplified when dealing with difficult people The DM is a little bit unique when it comes to connecting for a couple of reasons:

1. They may act like you are best friends almost immediately before you have any real time to connect.
2. It is not difficult to become "chummy" with these individuals if they like you, so these relationships

look promising in the early stages. However, cracking the nut and breaking below surface level is much more difficult with them than with most.

Here are a few tips for connecting with the DM:

* ❖ **Bring the energy!** DMs are full of life and they are attracted to others who are also. If you can be upbeat, fun-loving, and exciting, you are much more likely to catch their attention. Getting "on their radar" as another potentially engaging person for them to have fun with is the first step.
* ❖ **Show emotionality.** DMs are all about emotion. If you are stiff, reserved, and have your walls up, you will never connect with them. Share your feelings— good, bad, or otherwise. Be transparent (appropriate to your setting and role in their life).
* ❖ **Be spontaneous.** While many DMs are impulsive and sometimes to a fault, a moderated amount of this quality can make things fun. Showing a willingness to be flexible and doing things on the spur of the moment can go a long way with this personality style.
* ❖ **Compliment them** appropriately during the week and in front of their peers. Noticing them regularly and pointing out their legitimate contributions is a great way to make headway connecting with the DM.

Top ten tips for disarming a Drama Mamma

1. **Know their triggers and avoid them.** The DMs biggest trigger is getting ignored. Structure your offices, classrooms, seating assignment charts and other tasks with this in mind. If triggered, remember

this style tends to escalate quickly. Do your best to stay calm. The more worked up you get, the faster they will escalate.

2. **Feed their need to be the center of attention**. Give them their moment in the sun. Be cognizant of opportunities to recognize them publicly and in front of their peers. Remember private encouragement is not enough with these individuals. Their need is not just to be *affirmed*, but to get *noticed*. Let them be "king of the class" for a day. Allow them to make announcements. If they have the qualifications, put them in marketing, PR and other roles where they interface with the public and showcase their demonstrative side in likable ways. Recognize them formally at end-of-year corporate banquets or in front of your congregations.

3. **Provide a positive, upbeat work or classroom environment**. Although times to be serious certainly exist in all organizations, schools, churches, and personal moments, some cultures can be characterized as excessively negative, punitive or serious. These are bad fits for DMs. Do what you can to make your culture a positive one! If there are other "fun" people in the department, class or group, introduce them. When learning or projects can be accomplished via "games," step outside your box and creatively construct them.

4. **Provide opportunities to socialize**. DMs need regular, active human interaction. If you find it annoying that the pastor in your church asks people get up, greet everybody and shake someone's hand, remember this is meeting a need for people with the *I* style! DMs need that as part of their experience. Focus on *who* will be involved when explaining

projects. Create as many opportunities as possible in your classroom or corporation to work in groups. Have company get-togethers or class socials.

5. **Delegate the details when possible.** Because this personality style typically is not detail oriented, even if it is not completely possible, sometimes you can at least limit the details you make them responsible for. *I's* in general struggle with details and if you put an extreme version of this personality style in charge of them you are inviting a disaster. If you have hired or appointed a DM to a detail-oriented position you have identified the wrong person

6. **Depackage.** Because this style is prone to use vague language, break it down to identifiable specifics. "Instead of saying ASAP, I should have said I need you to check back in by ten o'clock."

7. **Validate what is valuable**. Verbalize what you *do* like about them and what value they bring to the table with their set of traits ("I appreciate your lighthearted approach to some of these issues—it is easy for the team to get bogged down in seriousness ...") before requesting a change. This reinforces the behavior you want. Remember, the more attention we pay to a behavior the more it changes. The following behaviors are ideal to encourage with this personality style: maintaining focus, working behind the scenes and it made them a hero, and avoiding impulsive acts to benefit them or their peers. Help them see the value of using restraint in certain situations and help connect with positive results important to them.

8. **Redirect to purpose.** After validating, remind them what the objective is. (*You are really funny, and I always like your sense of humor. In this meeting it's*

important that we accomplish ABC before noon.") A version of this can also be used when handling DM gossip. ("*I love talking to you—and that was a funny shift, but I like Suzie a lot and I have learned not to talk about people who aren't in the room—our purpose for this session was XYZ. I'd really like us to stay on task.*")

9. **Launch a preemptive strike against SOS!** Shiny object syndrome can get the best of any of us from time to time. But this "syndrome" plagues most *I's* and even more so the DM. So be aware that this applies to them ahead of time and act to circumvent it before it becomes a problem. Be specific when assigning tasks. Distribute work in small increments, provide regular check-ins and accountability, offer short-term incentives and ask for specifics. Your idea of that is probably different than theirs.

10. **Facts over feelings.** If a DM has caused significant enough problems to require confrontation, present them with facts. Allow them time to calm down so they can process what happened. Remember nobody thinks the most clearly when upset. And DMs get upset easier than others and feelings become the lenses through which they view events. Stress that "even though it feels one way, the facts are ..." "I know it feels like this to you ... but what I really need from you is ABC."

Speak their language

Now it is time to communicate strategically. Keeping in mind that communication involves a message sent plus a message received, and that beliefs filter both ends of the interaction, what factors are important to consider when preparing your BAM to deal with a DM?

Remember our five questions?

1. Who am I?
2. Who are they?
3. Who are they to me?
4. Who am I to them?
5. How might I need to adapt my natural approach to speak so they will listen?

So what would using these as a template to prepare for a conversation actually look like?

Consider an interaction from the example involving Shelly above. In response to her insensitive meltdown before prayer at the Bible study, several group members got together and decided she needed confronting. Cameron and Jennifer would initiate the conversation. Everyone recognized them as leaders of the group, felt they were spiritually and emotionally mature, and the girls found Cameron to be very good-looking (which the group knew would carry some weight with Shelly.) Jennifer would do the talking, so she was coached through the following questions:

1. Who am I?

Although Jennifer had never even heard of the DISC, it was identified that she had dominant traits in both the *D* and the *S* styles. She was extremely driven, had her own business, and perhaps had the most active social life in the group.

2. Who are they?

Jennifer and Cameron were dealing with a DM who had "out of control" *I* traits.

3. Who are they to me?

Because Jennifer and Cameron both had **D** and **S** traits, they viewed Shelly as a little annoying as a rule and highly inappropriate at that moment.

4. Who am I to them?

When considering this question, Jennifer and Cameron guessed that to Shelly, Jennifer was probably seen as likable, but a bit dominant and task oriented. Also, although almost everybody in the group liked and respected Jennifer, many of her actions were behind the scenes, so she wasn't a threat to Shelly's attention.

5. How might Jennifer need to adapt her approach to speak so shelly would listen?

When reflecting on this question, they realized that if Jennifer allowed her autopilot language to go unchecked, the conversation might have gone down a little like this:

Jennifer's S and D "Autopilot" Filters	Jennifer's Sending	Shelley's Filter	Shelley's Receiving
"Take charge immediately" / "Feelings of others should be prioritized"	"What you said to Stacie was completely insensitive and thoughtless—she was sharing something painful and you stole the show, shared something vague, and flopped on the floor."	"I must be noticed"	"Even if she is with a hot guy, who do they think they are minimizing my prayer request—I had just as much right to be heard as Stacie did!"

Jennifer realized that if she let her autopilot take over, she would probably come across as overly direct and use a tone of voice that was received as attacking and unsympathetic to Shelley's position. So she altered her verbiage strategically to speak Shelley's language. Her intentionally chosen words sounded like this:

Example BAM

B "Hi, Shelley. Cameron and I were reluctant to talk to you—we love how fun you can make the group ..."

A "But we know how important it is to you to be recognized by others—and it is really important to us that all in the group feel supported—and we don't want there to be any hard feelings on either side ... so we wanted to talk to you. We know deep down you are actually a very sensitive person, and we don't believe you intended to hurt anyone ... and that we want the group to continue to think highly of you ..."

M "So we felt like we needed to tell you that your actions at last week's Bible study really hurt Stacie's feelings ... not to mention rubbed a lot of the people in the group the wrong way."

What observations did you make regarding this BAM response? Was Jennifer as direct as she probably wanted to be? No, she most certainly wasn't. Did her protector instinct upset Stacey was hurt take over? Without hearing her tone of voice, one cannot be certain. However, the upset *S* in her was probably kept at bay or counterbalanced by not wanting to upset Shelley. The message focused on both Shelley's need to be viewed as noteworthy, Stacey's emotionally painful experience, and Cameron and Jennifer's desire for the group to feel supported. Even though he didn't actually say anything, having Cameron there did impact Shelley's response, as she did not want him to see her act off-puttingly

Setting boundaries and enforcing consequences

At this point the conversation could have gone one of two ways. The desired response would have been for Shelley to see the errors of her ways immediately, apologize and initiate a process of re-ingratiating herself to the group. In some cases, this happens in response to a BAM. When it does, boundaries and consequences need not be set, at least at this point. In this case, Shelley was moderately defensive and came back with a response of "Why do I have to be the one to initiate reconciliation—don't I have a right to have my time to share also?" So a modified revisit of this conversation was required.

Cameron then chimed in for the first time saying "You don't have to initiate anything, Shelly—it is completely your choice. And of course you have as much right as anyone in the group to share your prayer requests. We just saw how the group responded and didn't know if you were aware of how it came across to people. Although you are always welcome on Sunday nights, my guess is you won't get as many invites to future outside get-togethers if you don't say something."

Reviewing the guidelines from chapter 3, how did this conversation stack up?

1. Were Jennifer and Cameron clear about the boundary? Sort of. They all knew what happened, so in

this case the language was still effective. They determined that saying something like "*Interrupting a person who just shared that she had cancer to share a vague and secretive request that wasn't even about you and then flailing around on the ground is not a good way to make endear people to you*" would have been counterproductive. So simply referencing "What you did last week at Bible study," although not explicitly descriptive, was sufficient in this case.

2. Were they clear about the consequences? Yes. Simply put, she would always be welcome at the church-sanctioned Bible studies, but based on what they heard (and, although they did not explicitly say it, would practice themselves), she would not get invites to outside informal social get-togethers unless she showed some recognition of the effects of her behavior on others in the group. She would need to make some efforts to be more sensitive in the future. Remember, relational consequences are often the most powerful kind, not only for the extreme DM, but also for anyone with strong *I* or *S* styles.

3. Did they enforce the consequences? They did. Over the next month, the group didn't invite Shelley to three different social events. Although she did not initially respond, when she saw they were really serious, she did go to Cameron about "patching things up." A conversation was facilitated in which Shelley, to the best of her ability, apologized and asked what she could do to make it up. Shelley remained in the group for years to come. While she acted more reserved around certain people—more out of resentment than true repentance—she knew if she wanted attention, she needed to pick and choose the appropriate time to seek it out. Even

though she never completely returned to her old self, everyone else in the group could tolerate her much more moving forward.

Know when to walk away, know when to run

Answering the question of when to walk away always involves doing some form of cost-benefit analysis. When the cost outweighs the benefits, it may be time to cut bait. This decision can be a little bit tricky, because the best interest of everyone needs to be considered. What is in the best interest of the child may not serve the parent. What the company values, may not be best for a given individual. It is certainly possible that one partner in a relationship may be getting all their needs met, while the other is getting virtually none met.

In the example above, setting the boundary to essentially walk away until some changed behavior was demonstrated created a situation that was in the best interest of Stacy, who felt supported by the group. It was also in the best interest of the group, whose leaders strongly valued it being a safe place for people to feel validated and uplifted. Was it in the best interest of Shelly? Although she didn't see it at the time, probably. Just because my six-year-old twins don't know it is in their best interest to wear sunscreen on one-hundred-degree summer days, it still is. Shelley did at least change enough so she could continue to be a part of the group with minimal awkwardness. If she hadn't, it would have likely been necessary for the group to walk away from her completely. Even if that would have happened, Jennifer and Cameron at least did not enable her behavior, which would not have been in her best interest.

That doesn't mean she ever ultimately received the feedback in a manner that enabled her to make a significant change.

If I were here therapist or coach, that would be my goal. In this case, however, my loyalty was to Jennifer and Cameron, as they were the ones seeking my assistance. Although they wanted the best for her as well, Jennifer and Cameron's primary goal was protecting the health of the group at large. By having the conversation in the manner they did, coupled with their willingness to follow through, they could effectively disarm a DM and prevent her from harming future group members.

7

The Victim

We, the uninformed, working for the unaccusable, are doing the
impossible for the ungrateful.

—Jim Lundy

Mindset: "No matter what I do, bad things will always
happen to me."

Behaviors: Complaining, whining, blaming others, refusal
to problem-solve

Beliefs: I am helpless. The world is unfair, others owe me.

DISC parallel: One out of control manifestation of the *I*

Clinical parallel: Someone with *borderline, histrionic, dependent* and *narcissistic* traits.

Continuum

Mild	Moderate	Severe
I-------------------------I-------------------------I

Mild	Moderate	Severe
You have a tendency to blame others Rather than take responsibility Minor complaining and feeling Sorry for yourself	You cannot see others points of view. You get angry when you see others succeed. You don't work well with others cannot handle criticism	You take extreme measures to get others to notice how unfair life has been to you. You are bitter, entitled, and demanding

Description

The Victim represents a different out of control version of the *I* prototype on the DISC profile. This type is a little different than the other seven, in that, in clinical terms, people with *borderline, histrionic, narcissistic* and *dependent* personality traits can all exhibit Victim qualities.

It is again important to note that many people have some Victim traits who are not fully diagnosable with any disorder. In fact, when using this language to categorize a group of people it is especially important to have clarity about what we are talking about. Most of us have been *victimized* in this lifetime, whether in small ways or large. I had my wallet stolen at a concert one time. I have had my house broken into, my car window smashed in, and on one occasion I even had the lock of a hotel room I was staying at picked. Possessions were stolen on each occasion. I have had unfounded complaints made against me that hurt me temporarily. Some people have been shortchanged at the Wal-Mart and others have been raped. So all acts of victimization are not created equally. And we need to recognize that. It is important to remind ourselves that the *Victim* this chapter discusses is a *personality style*, in the same way that the other seven are. There is a big difference between someone who was legitimately *victimized* versus someone who maintains a *victim mentality*. People who are currently being or have recently been victimized and are having a hard time coping should be treated with the utmost compassion and supported in any way possible. They must be distinguished from perpetual whiners whose real or perceived slight may have been years ago, but continues to regularly assign blame elsewhere, regularly let you know how miserable they are, yet reject help, make excuses for their own unwillingness to take responsibility for present-day behaviors. John Maxwell made a pertinent statement while delivering a sermon that can serve as a powerful reminder to each of us in this area when he said, *"Don't let a single life experience become your entire life's experience."* So this chapter in no way aims to name-call or demean a group of people who have experienced legitimate trauma. It speaks to how to deal with those who maintain this victim mentality in a pervasive and long-lasting way.

When kept in check, personality features that acknowledge hurt and pain are valuable. They facilitate people feeling validated. These traits help students know their teacher "feels their pain" and gets the seriousness when they are bullied. They aid employees in feeling assured their supervisor will not allow hostile work environments to persist. Unfortunately, many people today would rather sweep things under the rug and pretend problems don't exist than acknowledge and deal with them. So our world needs people to point out legitimate issues and file complaints when they are necessary. Unfortunately, many leaders have enough *D* in them (as highlighted in chapter 4) that they have difficulty hearing legitimate constructive complaints and inaccurately label people as victims. The ability to be honest about negative feelings, hurtful situations, and problems is an admirable quality. Acknowledging and honestly dealing with hurts and concerns, whether in our personal lives, classrooms, or workplaces, is healthy and needed.

As with any trait, however, our biggest strengths can become our greatest weaknesses. And, unfortunately, the Victim's extreme nature brings out the downside of this set of traits. They blame, pout, and sulk. They accuse others of sinister intent. They demand sympathy, reject problem-solving, and refuse to engage in teamwork. They insist on their innocence and if you disagree with them, they get angry and defensive (i.e., *He made me feel this way—isn't he awful!*). Finally, few like to be put in the position of judge. To Victims, life is a drama playing out in front of them, and as Bob Leahy points out, this personality type assigns themselves the role of the Victim, someone else as the prosecutor, and asks you to rule on their behalf. This victim-perpetrator dynamic wears people out and rubs them the wrong way.

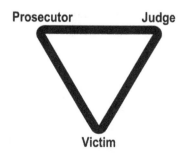

At their root, the Victim has been taken advantage of in the past and carries that into the present. As a result, she overestimates the "perpetrators" role in incidents and underestimates her responsibility. He also overestimates limiting circumstances in present-day lives. They are consumed with the pain from past wrongs and want others to notice it. They not only demand validation for perceived past wrongs, but they often seek compensation from others in present-day life for it. Some present a more "helpless" demeanor, while others come across as entitled believing that the world should take care of them because of it. When they don't, they get angry and feel more helpless. Any time they fail to achieve a given goal or desire, it is as though their internal doppler radar constantly scans for "evidence" of being wronged or experiencing an unfair disadvantage. By doing so, these perceptions are reinforced, and they condition themselves to believe further that there is no hope, perpetuating a thought process that attributes all negative in their life to the harshness of others. Clinging to this view enables them to maintain moral superiority, insist on their innocence in every situation, and refuse to take responsibility.

These beliefs drive several behaviors commonly seen in workplace, educational, church and other environments.

One such hallmark strategy of the Victim is eliciting sympathy. If you don't see the pain, they experienced they will try a little harder to "help" you see it. Coming to work or class with bandages, wraps, or walking with a fabricated limp is commonplace. The Victim is also the queen of the guilt stab. Has anyone heard this before?

"If you really care about me, you will pay for this for me?" or "If you understood, you would allow me this accommodation?" How about "I can't help but think that if I were a good mother my children would come visit their old lady more than once a month." Or "You know I have anxiety and can't get out and do anything for myself … If you really cared about me like a loving daughter should, you'd come pick me up every day."

This strategy is not isolated to Victims. However, guilt stabbing is a modus operandi to manipulate others for this personality type.

Refusing to take responsibility is one of the most common behaviors exhibited by Victims. Due to somebody else's behaviors, they cannot do homework, complete a project or do what their teachers ask.

Related to this difficulty with taking responsibility, the Victim regularly refuses to problem-solve. This type can be frustrating to work with. Even when presented with several plausible options, Victims will often come up with multiple reasons not to consider them. Even if you agree that something "shouldn't" have been done, this type remains committed to protesting the past and can't let it go and move forward. They are so focused on being validated for the problem that they are unable to investigate possible solutions. They are more interested in justifying their "stuck" position than they are changing it.

In addition to the more passive strategies described above, some Victims will want you to not only sympathize with them and see why they are not able to move forward, but also will take it a step further and demand that you give them special privileges to help them move forward. They demand special rules, special laws, or compensation. They can't take responsibility until someone else rescues them. However, this often produces a "catch-22" situation. If they receive help, then then they will no longer be sick/stuck. And if they are no longer sick or stuck, they are no longer deserving of the sympathy that drives them.

A final go-to strategy of the Victim is to up the ante. If you don't validate them sufficiently, they will often do something more extreme to make sure you notice how badly they have it. Remember the *I* needs to be seen. They need to be the center of attention. Victims escalating behavior to get you to notice this about them is a classic example. I have seen this almost become a game of sorts in the workplace akin to who can tell the biggest "fish story" but in this case the sickest one wins!

There is also an element of magnified or catastrophic thinking seen in the Victim and other people with *I* personalities. Albert Ellis called this "awfulizing." They adopt the idea that "I am the only one that has been through something THIS bad" and fail to see others have similar problems.

Ultimately, the Victim is so self-consumed with pain that it becomes his crutch. He views it as an asset and can't see the many ways it is not serving him well. Some such problematic Victim attitudes include:

- ♣ "Because of what I went through, others should feel sorry for me."
- ♣ "This is the worst! They are ruining my life!"
- ♣ "I shouldn't have been taken advantage of."
- ♣ "I deserve better!"
- ♣ "I have a right for you to feel sorry for me and not to move forward."
- ♣ "If I agree to problem-solve, I am saying what happened to me was OK."
- ♣ "If I move on, I can no longer hold them responsible."
- ♣ "If I agree to move forward, I give up my right to punish her."
- ♣ "If I agree to move on, I no longer have a right to ger him back."
- ♣ "Since nobody knows how bad my pain was, it's OK to do something dramatic to get them to understand."
- ♣ "I'd be successful if it weren't for others."

Again, you may believe one or more of the above at least to some degree. Remember beliefs are sometimes true, sometimes false, and often the "truth lies somewhere in between." Sometimes it is not a matter of right or wrong. Often they are simply matters of opinion. What one "deserves" could be approached from several points of view.

In addition to questions about "right and wrong" and "deserving versus undeserving," there is the notion of helpfulness versus unhelpfulness. This idea was taught to me in the most meaningful way by a Jewish woman in a group I led years ago. She was in her early eighties at the time and described fleeing from Nazi Germany in 1939. As she told her story detailing horrific acts she witnessed primarily done to family friends, there wasn't one person in that room who could argue that she did not have a "right" to be angry. However, the powerful truth she shared that day was that just because she may have had a right to become angry didn't make it *helpful* to stay angry. She shared that although it took her years to realize how she had unintentionally allowed this victim mentality to rob her of years of potential joy, she was truly set free once she did.

While not everyone's story impacts us so powerfully, the principle holds true across many contexts.

Even if everyone on your management team agrees with you that an incident was "unfair," the past is still the past and even though they didn't deserve this treatment, dwelling on the past is rarely a helpful approach. Regardless of how "valid" of a point the Victim raises, it is the leader's job to move the team forward in a constructive way.

The overarching tenet here is that Victims believe very strongly that because they had something happen in their past, that you need to recognize their pain, that because of it they are justified in not moving forward to complete the task at hand, and in extreme forms some believe they are entitled to be treated special because of it. To the degree that a person endorses this type of thinking, the more they will disempower themselves and decrease the likelihood that they will find success in the classroom, on the job, and in other areas of their lives.

Red flags

As with traits of every other personality style, you can always spot Victims ahead of time if you know what to look for. Here are a few red flags to keep an eye out for in different settings.

Victim red flags in the workplace

- ☐ Do they present for the initial interview in any way that sticks out? For example, are they limping, using crutches, etc.? If so, do they verbally bring attention to it or do you observe them watching you closely to see if you notice or comment on it?
- ☐ If the answer to the above is yes, and you ask them about it, pay close attention to how they respond. Specifically watch for overly blaming language or a dramatic or extreme presentation of the events.
- ☐ In the interview, ask them to tell you about a personal goal they achieved and one they did not achieve. As they describe the one they did not achieve, be on the lookout for language blaming other people for their inability to accomplish the particular goal in question.

- ☐ Do you observe whining or complaining regularly in the workplace?
- ☐ Does the employee demonstrate difficulty taking the initiative?
- ☐ Do they blame other current coworkers or supervisors when they fall short in a particular area?
- ☐ How well do they collaborate with others? Can they work proactively as a member of a team?
- ☐ Do they demonstrate attention-seeking behaviors on the job?
- ☐ How often are they late to work or calling in sick. Is there a pattern of family or life circumstance drama that is "out of their control" and constantly to blame?
- ☐ Does the person demonstrate a pattern of demanding special accommodations due to circumstances being "unfair?"

Victim red flags in schools

- ☐ Is the student frequently observed complaining, whining, or pouting?
- ☐ Do they regularly tattle on other students?
- ☐ Can the student take responsibility for their actions?
- ☐ Do they often use blaming statements such as "Suzy made me do it!?"
- ☐ Does the student have a pattern of drawing attention to herself by broadcasting accidents, wearing unnecessary Band-Aids, or faking injuries?
- ☐ Do they use the above injuries (whether legitimate, completely fabricated, or partially exaggerated) to get wanted time and attention in the nurse's clinic or otherwise gain favor or attention?
- ☐ How often are they tardy or absent? Do they have excuses with themes of blaming others?

☐ Do they constantly focus on "how bad they have it," or how hard something is and perhaps demand special accommodations because of it?

Victim red flags in personal relationships

☐ Are they overly sensitive and rigid when it comes to personal boundaries?

☐ Are they quick to make accusations about something that wronged them in some way? (They have a right to set whatever boundaries they wish to feel safe; however, when they get reactive or uncomfortable in response to statements or gestures that most people find benign, this should set your Victim radar off.)

☐ Do they use "guilt stabs" to get you to do something for them out of sympathy or shame?

☐ When recanting previous romantic relationships, can they see their role in why the relationships went poorly or at least identify something they could have done differently? Or do they place all the blame on their ex?

☐ Listen for non-responsible language in their complaining. Themes such as "they can't get a break in love" or "this is just the type of guy that finds me" are definite red flags for Victims.

☐ Do you note passive-aggressive behaviors, whereby the person doesn't honestly tell you (or someone else) that they are upset with you to your face, but engages in acts that will hurt you in some way behind your back?

☐ Does the person always blame siblings or peers, rather than see their role in the situation?

☐ When you are together, do they always seem to want to talk about how bad life is going or how they "can't catch a break?" Do they dwell on negative or hurtful experiences in their past?

☐ When you offer them encouragement or guidance, are they open to problem-solving and exploring options? Or do you find your encouragement to create positive change in their life constantly met with excuses and resistance, insisting they are helpless in the face of their circumstances?

A school example

Cole, a seventh-grader, was known among his peers as a whiner. He was not terribly disliked by his classmates but was a little immature and tended to pick on girls he liked in developmentally inappropriate ways. When his antagonism was not met with his desired response, he could often be found in the corner pouting or tattling to a teacher making something up about the person who did not appreciate his antics.

He became a regular in the associate principal's office; however, he did not respond to routine discipline in the same way many students did. When confronted by a school counselor, everything was someone else's fault, and he wouldn't take any responsibility for his instigating antics that often triggered him being sent to see her in the first place. It wasn't that he lied about what he had done; rather, he justified his actions by saying things like "other people do stuff much worse." He refused to consider any of the school counselors' feedback and was unwilling to problem-solve how to move forward more productively. Instead, Cole used the majority of his time with the counselor complaining about his peers and his teacher and how he could never do anything right no matter what he tried. Every suggestion his counselor posed was immediately shot down with reasoning that his teacher or a peer would never allow it to work.

A church example

Lisa was a woman in her forties who, in addition to her work with me, sought pastoral counseling for "help keeping her marriage together." When I asked if her husband Jim was open to coming in to discuss the problems together, she responded, "He isn't willing to do anything to help our marriage. I feel like I am unequally yoked; he won't come!"

However, when the pastoral counselor called Jim directly, he agreed to come in without any hesitation. When the appointment date came, Lisa was "sick" so Jim came in by himself. The pastoral counselor gave him several suggestions he said he was willing to try, including bringing Lisa to a marriage retreat they were having next month and attending a men's support group by himself. Although Jim followed through with the recommendations he was given, Lisa insisted on continuing to have appointments by herself. During these she did nothing but complain about how bad she had it, citing scripture verses to support her righteous lifestyle as well as verses that she used as evidence of Jim's unwillingness to keep his vows.

Although he had never mentioned it before, the day Lisa refused to go to the marriage retreat was the first time he actually suggested a divorce. He told the pastoral counselor it was the last thing he wanted, but that anything he proposed was met with a laundry list of things from years past being held against him. Jim's mentioning divorce triggered a response the pastoral counselor had not seen—one of desperation and vulnerability for the first time. During their pastoral counseling session that day, Lisa admitted that part of her hated the feelings of bitterness and resentment she had toward Jim and wished she did not have to live with them every day. However, she also acknowledged that there was a part of her that believed that if she tried to let them go and problem-solve for the future it would have meant that what he did was OK. Part of her was unwilling to give up her "right" to stay angry with him so she could continue to hold him responsible for something he did thirteen years ago. The pastoral counselor hypothesized that if she did this it might require her to give up her need to continue to hold things against him. Instead, she would need to consider taking a little responsibility on herself, which she was unwilling to do. Although he did not confront her with this hypothesis directly, because he did not believe she was ready to hear it, he did harken back to her use of Scripture and suggested that they look at verses on forgiveness together. After spending the first ten minutes of the session lecturing the pastoral counselor on the importance of living one's life according to Scripture, she could not very easily resist his suggestion. However, when they looked up a verse that said, "Love keeps no record of wrongs," Lisa again became immediately defensive. She retorted with "It's just hard to let go of wrongs when he won't do anything to help the marriage—I try to live a Godly life, but the devil just keeps after me, Pastor. I know this is spiritual warfare!"

Connecting with the Victim

Connecting is a foundational element of communicating effectively with anyone. And this truth is only amplified when dealing with difficult people. Here are some strategies that can be helpful for connecting with the Victim.

- ❖ **Compliment them based on their resilience**. Recognize they have been through a lot and overcome a lot. Stress the "overcome" part.

❖ **Validate what you can**. It is an important quality not to minimize pain—this helps people on the team feel understood and cared about. Remember it is possible to validate a feeling without complete agreement with everything they say. I have said to clients versions of "I don't blame you for being pissed ... It's hard to believe human beings do things like that to each other—humans can be just flat out terrible."

❖ **Normalize that most people get angry when victimized**. Most people get angry and probably want to get somebody back when they are taken advantage of. Validate that many feel this way, at least initially.

❖ **Use non-blaming language**. Language such as "I am sorry to hear that ended that way—I hope there are no hard feelings" is an excellent example of showing compassion without taking sides.

Top ten tips for disarming a Victim

1. **Begin with the end in mind.** This technique involves being especially cognizant of the idea explained in chapter 3 that "we teach people how to treat us." Many well-meaning but uninformed people believe that a compassionate approach is the answer for dealing with all people. An "end in mind" perspective with this group recognizes that this approach inadvertently fuels more Victim and attention-seeking behavior. Be direct. Be brief. And realize if conversations take too long, don't effectively elicit the behavior you desire, and drain you in the process, your approach is counterproductive.

2. **Acknowledge their suffering but move quickly to solutions.** There are multiple ways to avoid getting

sucked into long, unproductive tugs-of-war and time-consuming, energy-draining conversations. Validating a Victim's pain can play a vital role in disarming in the short term and connecting in a way that pays off in the long run. The key is to help them genuinely feel understood, and move on quickly. A simple statement such as "that sounds extremely difficult, what do you propose we do about it?" can go a long way.

3. **Grey rock method**. There was a deodorant commercial in the 1980s that became famous for the line "Never let them see you sweat." This is the idea behind the grey rock method. While this tactic can also be used with various types of difficult people, it can be extremely useful with the Victim. It involves communicating consistently in a stable, nonreactive manner and responding in an unemotional way that sends the message "everyone here gets same treatment regardless of the emotion you display."

4. **Roll with resistance**. This "drop the rope" communication technique can be a powerful way to disarm Victims by refusing to play their game. If their strategy to garner your attention and sympathy is to get you to see how much they need help but continue to refuse to accept it—what better way to disarm than agreeing with them that there really would be nothing you could do? "You are right. I really can't help you. There is no solution. This really will end in us not being able to complete this project and having to reevaluate everyone's position on the team."

5. **Mirroring**. Mirror back what they said or how they came across. Take a curious rather than mocking stance. Some Victims really lack the awareness to

see how they come across and this can help them gain insight. Those who want to change their behavior will.

6. **Shift from problem-focused to solution-focused**. Victim thinking is inherently problem-focused. One of the most challenging but most liberating things we can do for Victims is to empower them to see where their mindset is focused and help them make that shift. After validating, asking questions like "What would you like to happen as a result of this conversation?" can be extremely enlightening.

7. **Reinforce consequences**. Remember Victims are people oriented. Frame consequences in relational terms. Show them how their behavior turns people off and likely creates the opposite of what they desire.

8. **Deal with one situation at a time**. Like DMs, Victims tend to speak in globalizing language. Statements like "*It always ends like this*" are common ... Taking the particulars of a given situation is of vital importance. We can't change "what always happens." But we can change how we handle the task or relationship at hand. "I'm not talking about always. I'm talking about this project due Friday. What can we do differently this afternoon?" Shift their perspective to the here and now, look for an immediate "win" and take small, specified action steps to pursue it immediately.

9. **Don't ask why questions**. Sometimes these are unavoidable. But 90 percent of the time we don't have to go there. Like overanalyzes and Skeptics, "Why" questions are typically counterproductive for dealing with this personality style as well. Help them march on.

10. **Interrupt when necessary**. This will be harder for you if you score higher in the *S* or *I* traits. But this is usually necessary to utilize any of the above communication strategies. There are polite ways to interrupt. So give yourself permission to do it.

Speak their language

Now it is time to go a little deeper and communicate strategically. Keeping in mind that communication involves a message sent plus a message received, and that beliefs filter both ends of the interaction, what factors should you consider when preparing your BAM to deal with a Victim?

Remember our five questions from chapter 3?

1. Who am I?
2. Who are they?
3. Who are they to me?
4. Who am I to them?
5. How might I need to adapt my natural approach to speak so they will listen?

I helped the associate principal, Janet, consider these before having her BAM conversation with Cole one day in her office. We collaboratively came up with the following:

1. Who am I?

Janet had DISC-related training as part of their professional development workshop they had previously done with me, so she jumped quickly onboard with the approach. She could tell me that during her personality assessment process, *S* was the style she identified most strongly with. She described herself as "cheery," having a "positive attitude," and "a definite people person."

2. Who are they?

Having identified that Cole was a little bit atypical version of the *I*, we knew attention was important to him, he liked to be the center of attention, he felt he was entitled to his mindset, and he became pouty or otherwise disruptive when he did not get the attention he believed he deserved.

3. Who are they to me?

Having such strong *S* characteristics in her personality, Janet felt much more compassion for Cole than many of her educational colleagues who had become quite annoyed and put out by his behavior. She could identify with the "people person" in him and because of some shared qualities, she had to modify her delivery very little from how her autopilot would have communicated it.

4. Who am I to them?

Obviously, to Cole, Janet was first and foremost an authority figure. In his mind, he also associated her with punishment. Any time he got "in trouble," he went to her office. However, Janet also reported she frequently tried to cheer him up, make him laugh, or encourage him somehow. These words and behaviors were among the actions we examined to help her message hit its mark.

5. How might I need to adapt my natural approach to speak so they will listen?

Asking herself the question, "If my autopilot goes unchallenged, how would I likely send the message and how would he likely receive it?" Our educated guess surmised that it might look like this:

Janet's Strong S "Autopilot" Filter	My Sending	His Filter	His Receiving
"People must feel good"	"Cole, I'm really sorry that you are here again—what can we do to cheer you up? Focusing on what went wrong will only bring you down—you have a lot to be thankful for. Let's count your blessings and move forward!"	"My world sucks." "Life is unfair."	"She has no idea what I have had to go through. How dare she be positive and ask me to have fun and move forward with what I am in the middle of—she has no clue!"

We identified that Janet's natural positivity, even though coming from a place of compassion and desire to help, was being received as invalidating by Cole. I suggested that until he could properly read her intent, that she temper down the "cheeriness" and validate his feelings of "unfairness" related to his situation to connect with him before she showed any positivity or tried to "help" him. She said, "This seems weird—it feels like you are asking me to be more negative with him." In a sense, I was. So the BAM we crafted looked like this:

B "Cole, I know you have had it pretty bad this last year or two. I hate it that your parents are going through a divorce, and I know that you really want attention from the girls and you aren't getting much of it. I know life must feel pretty unfair to you right now. Since you don't get the attention, you deserve at home right now I don't blame you for trying just about anything you can to get attention here."

A "But I also care about you enough that I really want to see you succeed—and I would not be doing my job if I didn't point out that what you keep doing is not working for you. Not only are you not getting the laughs you hope for but when you pout afterward, you really alienate the kids whose attention you really want. Moving forward with a willingness to try to change some of these behaviors I am asking you to in the classroom does not mean that your hurt is any less important. I just want you to feel more included and recognized by people who matter to you."

M "Will you work with me to try to come up with some different ways to help you get what you want from the kids in the class?"

What did you notice about Janet's BAM? Was it overly flowery or positive? Was it oozing with warm fuzzies? Although her nurturing voice was likely an important part of this delivery, in terms of her content, she validated the struggle much more than the strong *S* in her naturally felt comfortable doing. Then she got right to the point.

This form of BAM cuts the chaff, immediately bypassing the surface-level behaviors. It communicates "I know the real you … The game is up!" Making this type of statement shoots straight to the core and immediately disarms the person then and there. Since this type of statement typically creates immediate awareness that "Oh my gosh—they see the real me," there is no longer a need to continue to wear the mask. The facade is rendered immediately useless and many times the person is willing to drop their guard immediately as they see it no longer has any value. Then and only then can they hear what needs to be said. The message here is simply "Can we have a real talk about ways we can work together to get some of your actual needs met?" If the answer is yes, you now have a green light to proceed with the problem-solving that was met with resistance on many previous occasions.

Setting boundaries and enforcing consequences

Different countries (as well as different school systems within countries) have different laws about what types of discipline can and can't be enforced. So, this section does not offer specific disciplines. But the important underlying principles remain the same. Be very clear with specific behaviors and consequences. Be willing to follow through. In this case, Cole responded well so no consequences were needed at this time. Ongoing conversations, however, focused on specific behaviors including interrupting others, arguing with the teacher, and leaving his assigned area without permission. Additionally, replacement behaviors were identified and worked on as well, including complimenting other students, taking a genuine interest in their words, and trying to decrease "whining" and pouting" "behaviors," including making loud noises, yelling, and isolating to the corner of the room.

Know when to walk away, know when to run

Again, specific school district policies often dictate what can and can't be done in terms of "walking away" as well. However, from a behavior change standpoint it is important to have negative reinforcers for problem behaviors. Remember we all teach people how to treat us. This is true in organizational settings, faith-based settings, and our personal lives. When I talk about this principle at my trainings and workshops, inevitably somebody gets mad. A teacher one time said, "I tried to tell him x behavior wasn't OK, but he just keeps doing it—we really can't make anyone stop anything!" I told her she was right. We can't stop anyone from doing anything—but we can stop them from doing it *to us*. Every time we refuse to set a boundary AND follow through with consequences, we are teaching that person "it is really OK to do whatever you want to me—I don't mean what I say." The problem in that woman's situation, as is often the case, was that she was unwilling to follow through with the consequences. In coaching, we identified consequences she was willing to follow through with that were permitted by her school district, including what "walk away" (several versions of detention) and "run" (suspending and expelling) strategies that she worked with her administration to consistently enforce.

Every time we fail to show students there are consequences for their actions, we are, usually unknowingly, encouraging kids to act in unruly ways. I have seen many schools that have come up with some wonderful behavior modification programs, utilizing both positive and negative reinforcement. But I have also seen school systems that have been unwilling to put the structure in place needed to foster a positive learning environment. In doing so, they often also inadvertently squelch motivation in previously inspired students that continue to be negatively impacted by a peer the school will not deal with. The reality is that some students need to be removed from class, suspended, or even expelled, for their benefit and the benefit of the other students.

8

The Landmine

"Be a mirror, not a sponge."

—Randi Kreger

Mindset: "I hate you / don't leave me."

Behaviors: Difficulty being or working alone, glamorizing a person or situation, enlisting others to come against someone they dislike

Beliefs: "Others will leave/reject me," "I must have the support of others"

DISC profile: One out of control manifestation of the *S*.

Continuum

Mild	Moderate	Severe
I-----------------------	I-----------------------	I
Sensitive, gets feelings hurt often, but recovers Around them uncomfortable	Mood swings severe Anger outbursts, impulsive	Enough to make others "Quitting" threats, lawsuits

Description

The Land Mine, (LM) or Eggshells Employee (whose name is borrowed from the international best seller *Stop Walking on Eggshells),* represents an overdeveloped version of the *S* prototype on the DISC profile; however, elements from the *D* and *I* can be seen in different people with this style as well. So in that sense, the profile of this person is slightly more complicated.

In clinical terms, this personality style often has traits of a person with *borderline personality disorder.* However, it is important to note that many people have some of these unpredictable traits who are not diagnosable with BPD.

People with this style are easily and frequently triggered, and they can go from zero to sixty in less than a second. When something doesn't go their way, it takes very little to set them off. When things in their environment are good, however, they can be full of energy and bring passion to the team.

When kept in check, these traits can enhance powerful dynamics in personal relationships and make for great team members. People with these traits can be passionate, creative and intelligent. They usually love working with people, as long as they are people they get along with.

On the downside, they are often known as the "overly sensitive" ones in the group or family as they can be easily triggered when comments hit them the wrong way. Oftentimes the person who commented has no idea what they said that triggered them. Thus, people who live or work with them often depict feeling like they are trying to navigate a Land Mine. They can also come to dislike people they previously thought highly of, and on occasions, very quickly. This person can then become a target of blame in their life and the resulting intense emotions can make for uncomfortable and tense work or social environments. As a result, LMs are prone to moodiness, typically have difficulty negotiating, and unnecessarily burning bridges. At times they even get punitive and can be known for filing grievances and frivolous lawsuits.

The friends, family members, coworkers, and teachers of these individuals never seem to know when they may step on a "Land Mine" and thus they have to "walk on eggshells" around them. Whichever metaphor you prefer, this personality type can be exhausting to deal with. For this reason, I have heard others refer to them as "emotional vampires." Even the most well-meaning person with these personality traits can be draining to be around.

As referenced above, LM personalities can be triggered suddenly and violently and unpredictably and can experience a wide range of intense emotions compared to the other types of HC individuals. Thus, they are much less predictable. For instance, the primary emotion Bullies exhibit is anger in response to being criticized. The Yes Man regularly gets anxious when someone's feelings are hurt. But the Land Mine can demonstrate guilt, fear, joy, shame, panic, hatred or many other emotions in response to various triggers. LM personalities not only feel a wide range of emotions, but they feel them extremely quickly and they feel them quite intensely. This intensity is one aspect of this type that exhausts the people around them. While some may act quite needy, others blow up in anger, while yet others feel hopeless when the slightest small thing doesn't go their way. And some people experience all of these! And sometimes it happens on the same day!

These mood swings may produce different behaviors

- ♣ Needy
- ♣ Yelling/cursing
- ♣ Panic
- ♣ Substance use or other impulsive, destructive actions
- ♣ Self-deprecating remarks
- ♣ Occasional self-injury

Another strategy of the LM is to enlist allies who agree with their point of view. Beware of them secretly recruiting team members or students to gang up on you if they disagree with you or if you have done something they perceived slighted them. In an honest moment of reflection to me, one client made the statement, *"Sometimes when I feel insecure it just helps me to go find someone else who will cosign on my bullsh!t."*

In the workplace, individuals with these personality traits exhibit high turnover from one company to the next. They not only burn bridges between themselves and their coworkers but also between themselves and their customers. Eggshell employees have often been described as "manipulative." "Manipulation" can be defined in different ways, but it is true that this type will go to great lengths to ensure they feel they have the relational support they need. Unfortunately, their misinterpretations frequently lead to hurt feelings. Their disproportionately intense emotions are a product of extreme thinking most people don't have. Some examples of such thinking include the following:

- ♣ "Since my teacher only complimented Sarah on her project, she must think mine sucks."
- ♣ "My boss didn't ask me to be on this project—he thinks I am a complete idiot."
- ♣ "Jenny didn't invite me to participate on the committee—I know she hates me."
- ♣ "The cute single guy at work, Seth, told me I looked nice today—What was wrong with how I looked yesterday!"
- ♣ "If I can't have everything I want, screw it! I am not even talking to you again!"
- ♣ "Since my husband doesn't call me back immediately, he isn't 100 percent committed to me."
- ♣ "Since I am so upset, it is OK to do whatever it takes to make the feeling go away."

Due to such erratic mood swings and impulsive and divisive behaviors, employers or school administrators commonly deem them as too high maintenance and end up firing or dismissing them. Because abandonment is a key theme with most of these individuals, dismissals and terminations rarely go well and bridges often get burned in the process.

Red flags

As with traits of each personality style, you can always find ways to spot LMs ahead of time if you know what to look for. Here are a few red flags to watch for in different settings in the early stages (prehire process, interviews, first days of class, etc.).

Land Mine red flags in the workplace

- ☐ What is the longest time they have held a job in the past?
- ☐ Ask them to describe the time they got the angriest on the job at their last place of employment.
- ☐ Ask them to describe a supervisor they worked well with in the past. Listen for extreme language and pay attention to the reasons they had for liking the person.
- ☐ Ask them to describe a supervisor they had problems with in the past. Listen for extreme complaints and be ready to discern how reasonable their explanation seems.
- ☐ Ask them to describe a conflict with a coworker. While this is a common interview question, intentionally listen to how they describe the conflict. Blaming others? Intense emotions?
- ☐ Ask them about a time they got upset with a coworker and, specifically, how they let it go and moved on to work productively with the person.

Assess their ability to move on in the workplace versus holding a grudge toward the person with whom they disagreed.

☐ Ask them why they left a previous job and listen carefully for their ability to blame others in extreme ways.

Land Mine red flags in schools

☐ Observe their present-day interaction with fellow students or teachers. Do you notice extreme mood or behavior changes?

☐ Do they seem fine one moment and shut down or withdraw the next?

☐ Do they regularly display angry outbursts, temper tantrums, or other disruptive behavior?

☐ Do they enlist classmates to "gang up" in some way on students they do not like?

☐ Are they chummy with a fellow student or teacher and then suddenly there is tension, or they are not on speaking terms?

☐ Do they seem to have constant chaos or turmoil in their personal life that causes them to miss significant time?

☐ Even if they are present in body, do they consistently seem to be upset and "somewhere else" mentally to the point that it affects their abilities to comprehend in meetings or classroom settings?

Land Mine red flags in personal relationships or settings

☐ Are you their best friend one day and the next day they refuse to talk to you?

☐ Do they seem excessively needy or controlling in relationships?

☐ Do they appear especially sensitive to rejection and describe feeling rejected by something you said when that was the furthest thing from your intent?

☐ Do you attempt to give a child or sibling some advice in a non-judging way, and they blow up and become immediately resistant?

☐ After a first date do they seem infatuated with you and after a second do they tell you they hate you and will not be calling you again?

☐ Do they seem fine one minute in a conversation and the next minute seem upset and you have no idea what happened?

☐ Do they regularly take compliments or even general communication the wrong way?

☐ Do you find yourself constantly having to explain what you "really meant?"

☐ Do you notice them "lobbying" to enlist other committee or congregation members to take their side against a particular person or issue?

A workplace example

Crissy and Irene had known each other for years. Their relationship had had some ups and downs, but there were periods they considered themselves pretty good friends. In fact, Irene even allowed Chrissy to stay in a spare room with her and her family for a few months while she went through a divorce.

Objective onlookers saw that Irene was likely jealous of Chrissy for several reasons, though neither one of them would acknowledge it. Irene had a reputation for being a little bit "moody," which contributed to difficulty maintaining relationships of various kinds throughout her life.

Crissy was currently in medical school and mentioned casually at a party she was looking for some part-time work to help pay her tuition. Irene, who had been working for years as a supervisor at a large retail outlet chain, overheard her and offered her a position with flexible hours.

In her third year of medical school, Crissy had an incident that required emergency surgery. Since she notified Irene she was on the way to the hospital and would need to get a high-risk procedure, Crissy was shocked to have three demanding voicemails requiring a "doctor's note" waiting for her when she was discharged from the hospital a few days later.

Although she obtained the note and took it in the day of her discharge, Irene refused to accept it saying she would get a demotion. The decreased pay did not meet her financial needs; however, she continued to work in that position for another two months, during which Irene was "all smiles" acting as if nothing happened.

Tired of feeling like she had to "walk on eggshells" around Irene, needing additional income, and concerned for the long-term effects on their friendship, Chrissy began interviewing for other jobs. She found a flexible opportunity with a local mortgage company. When Crissy notified the management team at the store, Irene begged her to stay, imploring her there was nobody who could do all she did for the store and she promised they would reinstate her previous pay rate. And besides, if she couldn't replace Crissy the regional manager would not be happy with her, and she could not afford to lose her job as she was now going through a divorce and was essentially a single mother. Having empathy for Irene's situation, Crissy agreed to turn down the job with the mortgage company and remain at the department store under the new conditions.

For the next two weeks Irene's mood was great. Other employees even noticed the difference. Some suggested she might have a new romantic relationship. Then, right as Chrissy started to feel like things might get back to normal, she came to work one morning to realize she was only on the schedule for three shifts during the following two-week period. When she approached Irene about it, she smiled and said, "Oh, you told me you wanted to quit, so I filled your position."

A relationship example

Suzie was twenty-eight years old and had been married for just over a year. Her husband, Neal, who thought he had found the love of his life, started to have second thoughts about marrying her after only three months of dating. Neal said, "She was so full of life. I loved her passion. I have never met anyone so spontaneous that made me feel so alive—but all of a sudden I feel like I am the devil. No matter what I do I can't do anything right."

Those who knew Suzie well knew she had a heart of gold, but she also had a reputation for being quite unpredictable and at times even volatile. Her coworker Amy said, "When she's in a good mood she's so much fun to work with. But you never know what will set her off—and if you do trigger her, look out!"

One day, she asked her if she would like to go out that evening with a group of them for a coworker's birthday. Amy said she just shut down and seemed angry with me the rest of the day but never said anything. "Actually, she did not talk to me the entire next week. Later I heard from a team member that when I invited her she got angry because we did not go out when it was her birthday."

Neal also relayed the story of a time he had asked Suzie if she cared if he went to shoot pool the following Friday night with his buddies. "She said it was fine that I could go, but when that Friday came around she kept hinting that she did not want me to and she ended up calling me five times during the three hours I was out. Since I didn't hear the calls in the loud billiards hall, she made me sleep on the couch when I got home."

Suzie's mother told me, "I love her to death, but if you say just a certain thing it will rub her the wrong way and you don't know what to expect. It feels like it comes out of left field, but we always seem to touch a nerve we did not mean to—and when we do, we pay for it for a while."

Connecting with the Land Mine

Connecting is a foundational element of communicating effectively with anyone. And this truth is only amplified when dealing with difficult people. The following strategies can be helpful when trying to connect specifically with the LM:

- ❖ **The struggle is real.** It is a common misperception that people with LM personalities manipulate emotion or purposefully blow things out of proportion. Making an accusation of this nature will almost certainly ensure you never connect with one of these people. Know that their emotions are real. They really do feel things that intensely! Some of this has to do with extreme thinking and some of it has to do with genetics. Even though some of us would have to "put on" to get to that extreme these are natural reactions for people with this personality. Don't minimize that.

* **Validate, validate, validate.** Bob Leahy said, "Not everyone is ready to change, but everyone is ready to be validated." I heard once that validation is the WD-40 of change. That is, perhaps we all respond better to requests after we have been "loosened up" in some way first. This is particularly true with LMs. The more validation you can give them on the front end, the more compliance you can expect on the back end. Validation must be genuine, however. Any attempt to use it manipulatively simply to achieve an end will be easily sniffed out and you will lose them immediately. Offer genuine compliments. Give them your sincere support. Let them know you are there for them, whether you are about to ask something of them or not.

* **Don't be "understanding."** This one is a bit tongue in cheek. However, many people with this personality type believe that you could never understand their pain because they usually have experienced more intense emotional experiences than you. So the mere words "I understand" are often enough to escalate an LM. It is common for well-meaning people who simply don't know what else to say, to verbalize something like this to comfort only to get the opposite result. Simply saying "I don't claim to understand how you must feel—what can I do to help so we can move forward," in an appropriate tone can be much more effective.

* **Smile.** This sounded goofy when I first heard it. However, research now supports the idea that even smiling itself can change a person's brain chemistry. Since people with LM are more sensitive to external

cues, this simple gesture can go a long way toward providing comfort in your presence.

Top ten tips to disarming a Land Mine

1. **Know their triggers and avoid them.** This may be more difficult with LMs than with any other type of difficult personality. The reason for this is simple: They can get triggered by so many things! Very specific triggers set off the other seven types, so it is easier to identify their patterns. LMs, as their name suggests, are inherently unpredictable. Nonetheless, the better you get to know your student, coworker, or employee, the more effective you will become at identifying some of their triggers.

2. **Feed their need for security.** Remember, the basic need of all *S's* is security. And the main belief in this specific version of the *S* has to do with the idea that others won't be there for them or support them. So stay after class with them. Answer all their questions about a project. Let them know you are available for support throughout the duration. Compliment them on tasks done well and people they helped or supported. Let them know you are there for them in any way you can.

3. **Provide stress reduction.** More and more companies are now offering yoga, tai chi, and other opportunities to reduce stress. Provide short breaks. Find ways your staff, teachers, or students can "recharge their batteries." While these kinds of personal proactive stress management routines reduce vulnerability to negative emotions in all of us, these can particularly help the LM. Every one of us gets our "buttons pushed" more easily when stressed out or

sleep-deprived. Consider how much more impactful this is for people whose buttons are more sensitive to begin with.

4. **Clarify meaning**. When you accidentally trigger them, it can be helpful to clarify your intent. When done tactfully, this can go miles toward disarming a situation that seemed destined to explode. Unfortunately, there are many ways to do this that are predictably counterproductive. A common one is to say "I'm sorry that you felt that way." While it is best to not apologize for something you really believe you didn't do wrong, this way of conveying that will inevitably be received as blaming and often escalate the interaction.

   Sometimes, a more effective approach is to say something like "Wait a minute—I hope you didn't think I meant ABC. What I meant was XYZ. I hope I conveyed that clearly." Go out of your way to let them know your intent and your heart behind the statement. Also using non-blaming terminology to wrap the discussion up can be helpful. "I am glad there are no hard feelings."

5. **Quiet their amygdala**. Don't worry. You don't have to be a neuroscientist. This simply has to do with facilitating their calming down. Trauma therapists all have several de-escalating techniques (soothing strategies, grounding exercises, distraction techniques) in their toolboxes to use with victims of traumatic events to help them calm down if they become emotionally flooded in the treatment process. Having some go-to tools to help people calm down can be extremely helpful in nonclinical settings as well. None of us thinks clearly when our emotions run high. Research on "mirror neurons"

shows us that others typically "mirror" our responses. If we escalate, they escalate. If we calm, they calm. Give them space. Find out what calms or soothes them. Refrain from giving them instructions or try to make a teachable moment out of an incident they have not yet calmed down from. Don't reward emotional outbursts in the classroom or workplace, but accommodate to the extent that you are able to help them regroup. Nothing productive will happen for you or them until you do.

6. **Generate options**. Most people seem to intuitively "get" that extreme thinking produces intense feelings. But one aspect of this "black-and-white" type of processing that is often overlooked is its ability to impact problem-solving negatively. Extreme thinking inherently limits one's ability to see shades of gray, or middle-ground options. When they can identify only two extremes, help them fill in the middle ground by brainstorming middle-ground options. Likely, one of those will offer the most effective course of action.

7. **The calm after the storm**. Immediately after a person with an LM personality style has an "emotional episode," there is always a time of calm following it and prior to the next time they get triggered. This time *immediately* following the blow-up is often the prime window for both confrontation and teaching. It is when they are the most malleable. So remember, if confrontation is needed, do so during this time following the quieting. Frame consequences in terms of peer rejection or write-ups.

8. **Manage moodiness (yours!)** Perhaps the number one key to dealing effectively with challenging people, particularly LMs is resisting the urge to respond to their reactivity. Instead, focus on your

personal development. Gain awareness about your own "buttons." Practice self-care. The more you can do to facilitate your mental well-being and manage your stress, the less vulnerable you will be to an LMs (or anyone's) intense emotional response.

9. **Don't do the splits**. There is a common term in the clinical world called *splitting*. Actually, you will hear the term "staff splitting" misused on many hospital units. This refers to pitting one person against the other. This is a hallmark quality of the LM. If you are dealing with a person with this style, it is important to ensure you communicate regularly with other significant people involved. That way, when a Land Mine says, "Well, she told me …", you will know better. Also, it is always OK to say, "That makes a lot of sense. Let me get back to you in a bit." Then you can check with the other person involved to ensure the LM hasn't manipulated you.

10. **Fight fair**. Some of the heinous things this style can do when they get mad can really drive you nuts. But remember, they are in your life for a reason in some capacity. So it is likely you have a stake in ensuring the relationship stays as healthy as possible. Resist the urge to stoop to their level or hit below the belt. We all know how that feels. And it doesn't make us want to give that person what they want.

Speak their language

Now it is time to communicate strategically. Keeping in mind that communication involves a message sent plus a message received, and that beliefs filter both ends of the interaction, what factors should you consider when preparing your BAM to deal with an LM?

Remember our five questions?

1. Who am I?
2. Who are they?
3. Who are they to me?
4. Who am I to them?
5. How might I need to adapt my natural approach to speak so they will listen?

So what would using these as a template to prepare for a conversation with an LM look like?

Let's look at an interaction between Neal and Suzie from above.

In response to her making him sleep on the couch for doing something she had provided her "stamp of approval" for, Neal prepared to broach the subject with his new wife by pondering these questions.

1. Who am I?

Neal was unfamiliar with the DISC, but we identified that he had a moderate number of *D* traits in his personality style. He wasn't overly domineering by any means, but did "get to the point" quickly and admittedly "am maybe not the best with thinking about feelings."

2. Who are they?

We had identified that Suzie fit the stereotypical definition of an LM personality. Specifically, she desperately needed the support of those she was most intimate with, would quickly feel desperate if she felt like she was losing it, and could be quite punitive when she felt emotionally slighted.

3. Who are they to me?

To Neal, Suzie was his new bride. He viewed her as his angel, but was quickly becoming quite disturbed how she could "flip a switch" and "become the devil."

4. Who am I to them?

After a little coaching from me, Neal realized that one of the characteristics of the LM personality, which is responsible for the mood swings, is a unique ability to shift one's view of others rapidly. He realized she viewed him similarly to how he viewed her most of the time—rather than angel, she called him *my prince*—but when she perceived he was not providing the emotional support she needed from him, this view would change rapidly, accounting for her anger and punitiveness.

5. How might I need to adapt my natural approach to speak their language?

Considering all of this, Neal realized if he allowed his autopilot language to go unchecked, the conversation might have gone down a little like this.

Neal's D Autopilot Filter	His Sending	Her Filter	Her Receiving
"Get to the point and get it done"	"It really wasn't fair that you were pissed at me the other night and made me sleep on the couch—you told me you had no problem with me going out that night."	"Loved ones must be there for me." "Others leave/ are not supportive enough."	"It is his job as my spouse to meet my needs. I needed him that night. He should have been available when I called. I had a right to make him sleep on the couch—maybe then he will see how he let me down."

We predicted that unless he altered his typically direct approach significantly, this conversation would not go well. Since he admittedly was "not always the most empathetic person in the world," and "she needs more empathy than most," that he would need to double down in this area. Although he started to understand how she thought much better, he still wanted to convey there was a problem with how this night occurred. While the conversation needed to happen, it also needed to be conducted to speak to her specific mindset. The BAM we constructed sounded something like this:

Example BAM

B "Hey, love—I wanted to talk to you about the other night. I know you need to feel supported in our relationship and I know I haven't always done the best job of that. I know you have been rejected in the past and I never want you to feel that way with me ..."

A "You mean the world to me and I want nothing more than to have a healthy, long-lasting, loving marriage."

M "For that to happen, I need to feel loved too. And I didn't feel that way being asked to sleep on the couch. Can we talk about how to do what we can to make sure neither of us feel that way again?"

What did you notice about this BAM response? This is a significant alteration from how the autopilot *D* in Neal would have wanted to say this. Also note that at this point, he does not even get into any of the specifics. He doesn't lecture her or make any attempt to "defend himself" at this point. Instead, he wanted to say things like:

- ♣ "You told me it was fine to go out!"
- ♣ "If you changed our mind you should have said something before I went."
- ♣ "You can't punish me for something you gave me permission to do!"
- ♣ "It's not reasonable to expect me to hear my phone in the bar."

Instead, his initial BAM simply seeks to open the door to have the conversation, and once she agreed, he could delve into some of these concerns.

Setting boundaries and enforcing consequences

Recall the guidelines from chapter 3:

Was Neal clear about the boundary? Fairly, but in a bit of a back door kind of way. This may or may not have been the case with Suzie, but some LMs will give people "tests" of sorts. One such test involves purposefully exhibiting emotionality so the other person will continue to back off. This is really an avoidance strategy some use to avoid unpleasant conversations. However, this isn't always the case. Many times, people with LM traits get triggered and experience genuine emotion. But there are times it is intentional, and when this is the case, it demonstrates the manipulative quality this personality type uses. This keeps others from setting boundaries with them and thereby controls the relationship.

If she had not given permission, even if she started to escalate, he would have calmly stated, "OK. I need to have this conversation, but it can wait until a better time if you like." By saying this, he is:

Showing respect for her wishes not to talk about it then. Again, he resists the urge to lecture and tell her what he thinks on his time frame.

He is also subtly setting a boundary. He is communicating that although he is willing to put it off if she isn't ready, the conversation still must happen.

So Neal, by being clear that he needs to have the conversation and will revisit it, is respectfully disarming this particular strategy.

Was Neal clear about the consequence? This was again vague, but intentional. This is the very essence of "walking on eggshells." While Neal knows in his mind, he is not going to tolerate these behaviors the rest of his life if nothing changes, he is being careful about how he states this so as not to trigger Suzie at this moment that he is trying to create some positive momentum. A subtle consequence is again suggested by the language "healthy, long-lasting, loving marriage." This implies, in a compassionate way that makes every effort not to trigger her, that the marriage will not last if certain behaviors continue.

Did Neal follow through? In this case, he did. The next evening when Suzie had calmed down, he broached the subject again by asking, "When is a good time this week for us to talk?" Again, this is time-limited. It says, "We will talk this week—when during this acceptable time frame is good for you?" The conversation happened the next night, and Suzie was extremely remorseful. That did not mean similar interactions did not continue to happen, but they occurred less frequently. And when they did, their willingness to have this difficult initial discussion provided a foundation and a basis for continuing to work on their relationship.

Know when to walk away, know when to run

Although people with LM personalities will always be more reactive than most, many are willing to change their behaviors. Remember, the *S* is the strongest trait of this type, so relationships are of the utmost importance. So when they see a relationship might be at risk, many are willing to make the changes necessary to maintain meaningful relationships. However, there are times it is best to walk away. When Neal approached Suzie intentionally and compassionately, she was willing to have the necessary conversation. Aside: NO LM will be willing to have conversations requesting behavior change while emotionally charged. MOST will be willing to once they have calmed down. So timing as well as approach is important. Once you ensure you have done your part on both of those fronts, if the person is still unwilling to budge, it may be best to walk away. There are two obvious times this is the case:

1. Even after you have done your part, some extreme LMs will never be open to feedback. If they are not even open to having an initial conversation, the likelihood is poor you will see movement.
2. A second time it may be best to walk away is when the person IS willing to have the initial conversation, verbalizes remorse, but is unwilling or unable to change the behavior over time.

Many people can't recognize their problematic role in communicating and are quick to blame the LM. And the reality is that when you don't know how to speak their language, you have virtually no chance. But when you have equipped yourself with the proper communication skills, many people with this personality type can be reached. However, as with all types of HC people, there is a small percentage you will need to break up with, fire, divorce, remove from the classroom, or otherwise separate yourself from them.

9

The "Yes Man" (or "Yes Ma'am")

"I am thankful to all the people who said no to me.
Because of them I can now do things myself."

—Albert Einstein

Mindset: "Everyone must be taken care of."

Behaviors: "Nurturing, sacrificing, and caretaking behaviors. Saying yes when it is in their best interest to say no.

Beliefs: "I must put others' needs before my own."

DISC profile: One out of control manifestation of the *S*.

Continuum

Mild	Moderate	Severe
I------------------------I------------------------I		
Sensitive, gets feelings Hurt often, but recovers	Mood swings severe Enough to make others Around them uncomfortable	Anger outbursts, impulsive "Quitting" threats, lawsuits

Description

n clinical terms, the "Yes Man/Ma'am" (YM) often has *dependent* personality traits. This represents another out of control version of the *S* prototype on the DISC personality profile. YMs, as with all *S's*, are social, loyal, and friendly. They routinely sacrifice their needs for the well-being of others.

When kept in check, these traits make people feel comfortable. They can be great spouses, teammates, and confidants. These are the people you pray to have in your life during a personal crisis. They welcome you at parties. They help you feel comfortable at uncomfortable socials. If you need help on a project for school or work, the YM is exactly who you will love to have sitting next to you. If you ask for help, you are sure to get it!

Many wonder how a person who is all about *avoiding* conflict and the uncomfortable feelings associated with it makes a list of "difficult" people in the first place. In some ways they *are* drastically different than the seven other types. However, they can be "difficult" in their own ways.

On the downside, YMs come across as needy, whiny, and annoying. It can be quite draining and distracting to work with a person who always needs someone by their side, constantly asks questions, and can't seem to do anything on their own. They often say yes when it is in their (or your) best interest for them to say no. Because they always put people before tasks, they can be disorganized. It can be challenging to supervise someone who is constantly telling you yes, but then getting sidetracked in personal conversations and never actually following through to complete the task. In dating relationships, clingy partners can drain you of your energy. Overly needy members of congregations take up disproportionate amounts of managers' time. And in business the individual with no spine is often experienced as off-putting.

Additionally, people with these traits who have trouble saying no have trouble meeting deadlines because they get pulled away at someone else's request. In fact, many supervisors will report their biggest "headaches" are not people who push back. At least they know where they stand. Rather, many will report it is those who tell them yes to their face, yet have difficulty completing a task without constant supervision. On the flip side, managers with too many of these traits tend to see only the positives in others and will miss problem behaviors that need to be dealt with in the workplace. Failure by key management staff to address problem behaviors between coworkers leads to employee turnover.

YMs tie their entire identities to the support and approval of others. They love being with, talking to, and communicating with other people. They thrive off verbal affirmation. They need physical touch, and they live for support and human connection.

People with these personality traits have difficulty being alone or having extended periods of time with a lack of personal contact. Excessive texting, spending hours on the phone, and loads of time together in person with friends and family is commonplace for this type.

Like the LM, in romantic relationships, YMs tend to become attached extremely quickly. However, unlike the LM, YMs typically hold stable and long-lasting relationships, whether healthy or not, rather than short-lived and volatile ones. Due to their inherent submissiveness, they end up finding themselves with poor partners or friendship groups, compromising their moral values to "fit in."

Also, people with this personality style exhibit behaviors, often outside of their awareness, that facilitate this rapid attachment. One time, I suggested to one of my clients who just got out of an unhealthy romantic relationship, to "move slowly" when she told me she had already started seeing someone new. This interaction was memorable because in response to this suggestion she looked at me like I had three heads! She said, "I have no idea what that would even look like."

Excessive texting, phone calls, time spent together in person, sharing too much too soon, immediate physical or sexual contact, and cohabitation are all among behaviors that facilitate attachment at an expedited and arguably unhealthy pace. These are all choices people make. As silly as it seems to some, thousands of individuals like my client don't have the awareness to realize this phenomenon has played out over and over in their lives—due to a series of yes decisions on their part.

Even high-functioning people in relationships can suffer from this tension around independence versus dependence. The more dependent partner may constantly find themselves saying things like "I don't feel like I'm getting my needs met," "I need more quality time," or "Why do you want to spend so much time with your friends?" On the flip side, the more independent partner typically says things like "I need a little alone time," "I think we should also have our own hobbies," and "Do you always have to have your hand on my arm in public!"

Outside of workplace and romantic relationships, these traits can cause considerable problems in family, community, and church relationships as well. Problems related to these traits can rear their ugly heads particularly in faith-based communities that laud sacrifice at all costs. While many consider some of these behaviors admirable, some people within the religious community could benefit from hearing that being a servant does not mean being a sucker. In fact, taking care of oneself is necessary to be healthy enough to help meet the needs of others. There is a reason flight attendants, in their preflight spiels, state some version of "please secure your mask before assisting those around you." They know that if you are incapacitated, you will be in no shape to help those around you who may need it. Unfortunately, many people involved in the church end up overcommitted, stressed out, and resentful.

A final characteristic of this style is that, also similar to the LM, they get their feelings hurt much more often than the others. Unlike the LM, however, rather than erupt or do something erratic, YMs typically shut down or go find someone to encourage them. While emotional sensitivity is a trait that we now know some people are born with predispositions to, those with this personality would do well to learn that just because somebody says something does not make it true. And even if it was, approval from that particular person is not vital to their survival.

Some examples of YM attitudes can be seen in the following statements:

- ♣ "Since she asked, I have to help."
- ♣ "Saying no is rude."

♣ "If I say don't always say yes, I will be a disappointment to my family/faith."
♣ "If I don't ask, I might do it wrong and lose the approval of others."
♣ "I need to get all the help I can to be sure I don't let others down."

It may seem strange to some that these attitudes have to do with *seeking* help from others while different attitudes have to do with *offering* help to others. People unfamiliar with personality dynamics mostly don't realize that individuals with approval-seeking and dependent traits can manifest in different ways. In her international best seller *Codependent No More*, Melanie Beatty describes a pattern known as the enabler-dependent cycle. The dependent in the cycle is the easy one to figure out. He or she is the one who may even be addicted to a substance, a behavior, or a person and is overly reliant on him/her/it for survival.

The enabler is the one who continues to intervene on their behalf, "rescuing" them from the consequences of problematic behavior. These rescuing behaviors prevent the person from learning the lessons they need to learn to change their thinking and behavior. But here's the catch. Enablers often view themselves (and may be viewed by others) as the "strong" one—the superhero who is always there to help in times of need. But what many fail to realize is that, while counterintuitive, THE ENABLER IS JUST AS DEPENDENT AS THE DEPENDENT! If you examine that person's life, they will almost assuredly have a pattern of finding "damaged" people to fix, serve, or even date. The bitter pill to swallow is that the enabler is really just dependent on having someone to be dependent on them. As the old joke puts it: "What happened when the enabler almost fell off the cliff? ... Someone else's life passed before her eyes!"

The bottom line is that this personality style may engage in excessive giving *or* taking. And this style inevitably attracts a certain type of person to them.

In "The Sponge" episode in season 7 of *Seinfeld*, Jerry jokes, "I am a taker; I have to be with a giver. If everyone is taking, no one's giving—it's bedlam!" While it was funny in that context and by that actor, that very dynamic plays out like clockwork in relationships and workplaces all over the world. These traits may seem relatively harmless compared to many behaviors seen exhibited by other types of difficult personalities; however, they pose significant problems for not only the YM but also those around them.

Red flags

As with traits of each personality style, you can always spot YMs ahead of time if you know what to look for. Here are a few red flags to keep an eye out for in different settings.

Yes Man red flags in the workplace

- ☐ How much do they talk in the initial interview?
- ☐ Ask them to describe a project from a previous job in which they had to enlist help from somebody else. Listen for a natural deference or inability to complete tasks independently.
- ☐ Ask them to describe a project from a previous job they did start to finish by themselves.

☐ Listen for a lack of assertiveness or a difficulty describing such a situation.

☐ Ask them to give an example from a previous job of something they took on of their own initiative. Listen for YM traits.

☐ Do you observe them getting distracted from projects regularly due to socializing with coworkers?

☐ Do others report it is difficult to get work done with and around them due to excessive talking and asking of questions?

Yes Men red flags in schools

☐ Do they have difficulty completing class assignments in the classroom due to talking to friends instead of working? (Not just being easily distracted—but due to a need to be constantly talking to others).

☐ Are they capable of taking initiative or showing leadership in the classroom?

☐ Are they easily influenced by peers to go along with decisions they would never make on their own?

☐ Do they need an inordinate amount of encouragement to complete assignments they are clearly academically capable of completing?

☐ Do they tell teachers that yes they understand directions even when they don't just to avoid disappointment from the teacher?

Yes Men red flags in personal relationships

☐ Have they stayed in unhealthy or abusive romantic relationships in the past for long periods of time because they were afraid of being alone or unable to stand up to the individual?

- ☐ Have they failed to move out of their parents' house by a developmentally appropriate age due to lack of independence or responsibility? (Not temporary stints of moving back in for financial or nondependent-related reasons).
- ☐ Do they have a history of immediately seeking new romantic relationships immediately when the previous one ends?
- ☐ Were they incapable of remaining single for extended periods in between dating partners?
- ☐ Do they avoid pursuing friends, hobbies or interests outside their immediate family or romantic relationships?
- ☐ Do they constantly text or call or want to spend excessive amounts of time together in a manner that feels draining to you?

A personal example

Andi always described herself as a people pleaser, and she viewed it as a good thing. "Everyone around me knows that they can count on me," she said proudly one day. If her boss asked her to stay late for no extra pay, she said yes. If they were running short on volunteers at church, they knew who to call, and Andi would say yes. And if one of her friends needed someone to call in the middle of the night, everyone knew, she would say yes. Andi was the "go-to gal."

Being everyone's YM became a problem as she started saying yes when it was in her best interest to say no. She told her supervisor yes, she would take on an extra task when she knew she would not have time to get to it. She said yes to going out with her friends when she knew she needed to stay home and study. She said yes to her helping her mother clean out her closet when she promised her husband, they could go out on their first date night in over three months. She said yes and agreed to volunteer at the food bank the evening before her taxes were due. What Andie viewed as a positive personality trait hurt her finances, credibility at work, and most importantly to her, meaningful relationships.

A church example

Mark lived in a large city where he participated in a church singles group of around two hundred people in their twenties and thirties.

While the group did have some cliques, as most large groups of various kinds do, it was fairly inclusive and seemed to have a place for people at just about all stations in life. Not being overly athletic nor having the best social skills, Mark was viewed as a bit of a "misfit," at least within popular circles of the group. He played on the church league softball team but was the worst player on the team. He participated in all the social events, where he frequently struggled to get the attention of a certain woman in the group. To his credit, he often approached women at the functions, unlike many of the guys who were too shy; however, his awkwardness often caught the attention of nearby members of the group. Mark desperately wanted to be liked by the popular crowd and could usually be found hanging out around them at get-togethers. He even crashed a few personal parties he was not invited to.

One year at a men's retreat, a conversation broke out late at night outside a cabin over a campfire about several women in the group. Guys shared in confidence their thoughts about the various ladies in the group and particularly mentioned women they were interested in asking out.

The very next week in Sunday school two women in the group, Jill and Angie started teasing one of the guys, Aaron, using information they could only have known if they were sitting around that campfire circle the weekend before. Completely embarrassed, Aaron immediately went to a core member of the group sitting outside the cabin that night. The rat was immediately obvious to the group. It meant so much to Mark to have a couple of select woman in the class pleased with him for providing "insider knowledge" that he was willing to betray the confidence of the guys who shared in fellowship with each other that evening. Similarly, anytime one of the attractive women in the group moved, he was the first to show up at her apartment with his newly purchased truck to help lead the moving efforts. It should be noted that when any men (or unattractive women) in the group needed help moving something, he was always conveniently "unavailable." This not-so-subtle pattern became known as the "Mark McKinley moving ministry" secretly among the group. Mark's willingness to do anything to get others to like him cost him his reputation in the group and ultimately led to social suicide—unknowingly creating the scenario he feared the most.

Connecting with the Yes Man

The YM is perhaps the easiest of this group of difficult people to connect with. In fact, as noted above, since they often do everything we want them to do! Although you may not need them, the following strategies may be helpful when connecting with the mindset of the YM.

- ❖ **Provide nurturing**. If you have some *S* in your personality style this will likely come easier for you. If you don't, try your best to demonstrate a little with the YM in your world. For people with this type, a little nurturing goes a long way.

❖ **Offer reassurance.** This style constantly needs to be told they are doing well (when they legitimately are). Let them know you value them and you are there for them early and often. It is easy to experience this type as "needy," and feel exhausted interacting with them. This is why they are difficult. Be thankful you are not dealing with some of the traits of the other seven, which can be much more troublesome. Continue to offer encouragement on a regular basis.

❖ **Be a friend.** Allow them to talk and share their personal stuff. They may need a lot of reassurance but they also can offer a lot of reassurance. Allow them to encourage you and others. Small talk and a little personal chatting can go a long way to show them you are human too. They can be excellent conversationalists and fun to talk to many times as well.

Top ten tips for disarming the Yes Man

1. **Know their triggers and avoid them.** YM personalities lack initiative and assertiveness. Limit their decision-making. Provide a stable, steady environment with authority figures present or make them easily accessible. Assign responsibilities to the YM for only small amounts at a time. Assign someone else on the team to be responsible for having tough, confrontational conversations.

2. **Slow it down!** If you have a fair amount of *D* or *I* in your personality, moving fast is likely an element of your personality you may not be aware of. Be intentional about slowing down for this style. They need it to feel comfortable in the environment and

cared for by you. Going too fast or talking over people when orienting, going over classroom rules, or generally providing early expectations is my best advice for how to lose a YM right off the bat.

3. **Feed their need for people.** Remember, not only does this style fall in the *S* category of personality, but they are an extreme version of it. All people need people. But the reality is the YM needs people more than most. Provide opportunities for them to work in groups when possible. Allow small amounts of regular socialization so long as it is not disruptive to the classroom or work environment. Make them aware of extracurricular activities or provide opportunities outside the office to get their social needs met.

4. **Provide reassurance.** More than any other, this personality style thrives on positive strokes. Ask them if they need help or if you can do anything for them regularly. Check in to ensure they don't have any questions about assignments. Assure them you will be there to help them at any point in the project. They may even say no but asking regularly helps them feel safe in the environment and supported that you "cared enough to ask."

5. **Tell them what to do.** This would be terrible advice for dealing with someone with *D* or *C* traits. Many people have control issues to one degree or another. But this particular style feels some comfort when receiving directives. They will likely never have leadership or management jobs, and often find their ways to more subservient occupations or roles. On the bright side, this makes them teachable, coachable, and open to accountability.

6. **Provide clear expectations specific actions steps, accountability and deadlines.** YMs will stay within

the boundaries if they know what they are. Their sin is not purposeful defiance. But similar to DMs this style can get distracted from the task at hand. Be clear about what you expect. Give them specific action steps with deadlines. Teach them how to focus and follow through. Doing this reassures them and they will often follow through to please you. So giving such directives does not trigger this type in ways that it does others. And due to their tendency to say yes to the nonessential tasks that detract from the mission, deadlines are often necessary.

7. **Let them know it is OK to be honest.** This is when the YM can be a problem. They care so much about what others think that they often won't be truthful for fear of hurting someone's feelings. Give them permission to tell you the "whole truth." Let them know failure to do so will hurt your relationship with them and damage your trust in them. Facilitate an environment conducive to honesty. Encourage it. Model it. Intervene when other team members or students act in ways that reinforce it. The "*if I tell the teacher the truth, others will call me a rat*" mentality is rampant in schools. Sadly, many teachers get so overwhelmed and can be ill-equipped to deal with it that they often would rather not hear it either. Thus, many well-meaning educators (and other leaders) reinforce and enable this problem due to these traits.

8. **Appeal to their need for approval.** Since YMs are extreme versions of the *S* style and relationships are of the utmost importance. Tell them how important your "ask" of them is to you. Use personal language such as "Can I count on you to do to do that for me?" Convey consequences in relational terms as well. Help them see how their choice, as caring as

it was toward one person, also let down many others in ways they did not recognize.

9. **Venture a guess!** Some YMs are no responders. That is they never seem able or willing to answer at all! Ask open-ended questions. Don't give them an opportunity to just answer yes or no and shrug their shoulders. If they say, "I don't know," counter with "what's your best guess?"

10. **Express sincere appreciation**. After you tell them what to do, let them know how much you appreciate it. Note that this is different from recognition. DMs need to be the center of attention. They need others to see they were recognized. On the other hand, YMs don't need, and sometimes would even feel uncomfortable with public recognition. A kind word or a pat on the back behind closed doors means the world to this type.

Speak their language

Now it is time to communicate strategically. Keeping in mind that communication involves a message sent plus a message received, and that beliefs filter both ends of the interaction, what factors should you consider when preparing your BAM to deal with a YM?

Remember our five questions?

1. Who am I?
2. Who are they?
3. Who are they to me?
4. Who am I to them?
5. How might I need to adapt my natural approach to speak so they will listen?

So, what would using these as a template to prepare for a conversation look like?

Consider the following interaction Andi had with her supervisor Ron, at one of her performance reviews. Ron met with me for coaching in preparation for the meeting, and we reviewed the formula collaboratively, having Ron ask himself the following questions:

1. Who am I?

One of the reasons Ron needed coaching in the first place was due to his combination of strong *D* and *C* traits. He was extremely task oriented, driven to achieve excellence, and intolerant of difficult behavior.

2. Who are they?

We knew Andi was a YM who had out of control *S* traits. She was the reason the term "people pleaser" was invented.

3. Who are they to me?

To Ron, Andi was a "difficult" person. While most of the team viewed her as highly engaging and likable, Ron viewed her as a nuisance whose talkativeness was an impediment to the team.

4. Who am I to them?

Ron had never stopped to ponder how Andi viewed him. Frankly, he didn't care. He had gotten away with not caring for years until new management recently took over the company and brought a new culture to the organization. Because he had grown so accustomed to the old regime, he resented taking this extra step, but saw the importance of keeping performance high and morale strong. So he was at least willing to entertain the idea that Andi likely viewed him as an old curmudgeon in the vein of Ebenezer Scrooge.

5. How might I need to adapt my natural approach to speak so they will listen?

Asking himself the question, "If my autopilot goes unchallenged, how would I likely send the message and how would she likely receive it?" our educated guess is that it would have looked something like this:

Ron's D and C "Autopilot" Filters	His Sending	Her Filter	Her Receiving
"Do things well" "Do things fast."	"You talk too much. You need to do what you tell me you will do and get to it as soon as you tell me you will. If you don't get with the program, we will have to find someone more interested in doing what they are told."	"People's feelings are the most important thing"	"I don't fit in here. He doesn't like me and I can't even talk to my friends. Maybe I should find somewhere else to work."

It was apparent very quickly that Ron's autopilot would not have gone over well with Andi. It didn't go over well with the rest of the staff either. So, it was bound to be a disaster talking to any YM. Ron, surprisingly, was willing to change his approach to Andi. His BAM sounded like this:

195

Example BAM

B "Andi, I really appreciate you taking on some of the extra projects I have given you this past quarter. Your extra efforts have really meant a lot to the entire management team and we wanted you to know this. As you can see from the left column, we are pleased with your work in almost every area."

A "Because you are so valued by this organization, and you bring strengths of encouragement to this team lacking by many in this company, myself included (sarcastic, self-deprecating chuckle) I need you to hear one thing. I know you care about encouraging your team deeply, and this is mostly a strength ... We do need more people with this quality ..."

M "However, as you will note in the right column, there are times I assign you tasks and you are quick to tell me with a smile that you will do them, but then you get distracted talking and don't get them done. This leaves us in a bad spot. So the one thing I need you to focus on is completing tasks given to you in a more timely manner without getting distracted talking to others—this would really help the whole team achieve their goals if you could move in this direction. I'll be glad to continue to assign you group projects so you can work with your friends as much as possible if we can work to improve this one area."

What did you notice about this BAM response? Did Ron scold her like he wanted to, ignoring all her positive contributions in lieu of focus on her "chatty Cathy" side? No. In as nurturing of a voice as he was capable of, he affirmed all the things she did well, then also pointed out the problematic area of excessive socialization on the job.

Setting boundaries and enforcing consequences

In the above example, Ron didn't set a firm boundary because he hoped Andi didn't need it. He hoped the positive reinforcement of continuing to be allowed to work in groups with friends "if we can work to improve the problem area" was enough. In this case her response fit the classic YM pattern. She was extremely apologetic and grateful during the conversation. Although we cannot read her mind or heart it is likely her response was genuine at that moment. With this type, they usually are. However, in the subsequent weeks, the problem did not get better. Although Andi likely had the best intentions, she appeared to lack the awareness that she continued to accept invitations to visit with coworkers rather than focus on her assigned tasks. There also appeared to be other occasions when she *was* aware of a need to stay focused on work, but (because she had taught others how to treat her) was approached with others personal problems and allowed her helping instinct to override the importance she placed on immediately following up with what Ron had asked her to do.

Due to this, six weeks later a follow-up discussion was already required. Prior to the meeting, Ron again reviewed his five questions. He would have to be more direct with his BAM this time, but he needed to guard against allowing his autopilot from completely taking over the conversation. His approach still needed to be a little more measured than he would naturally take. It sounded like:

B "Andi, I hate it that I have to have this talk again so soon. Again, I want to affirm how valuable it is for us to have someone so encouraging on the team."

A "And again, I want to let you know the reason we are talking is because I really want you to be able to succeed on this team."

M "But it has come to my attention that the visiting with coworkers for extended periods of time that we talked about at your performance review only six weeks ago has continued to be a problem. I heard Beth call you over and start talking to you about her boyfriend. I know that you were concerned with her and wanted to help her. But your decision to spend an hour comforting her kept you from doing what I asked you to get done before you left work that day. And Jim and Melanie couldn't do their part until you completed yours. So you really let the team down.

"I was hoping you could change this on your own. It disappoints me that you couldn't. So I am now going to have to give you assignments to complete on your own for a while with specific deadlines. I will check in with you to be sure you have everything you need, and my door is always open, but I need to see you start meeting deadlines for the next six weeks. If you meet these deadlines, we can revisit having you return to the work groups. But if you fail to meet the deadlines, I may have to consider moving you to products, which you know would mean a wage reduction and working with a new team. Do you have any questions?"

What do you notice about this BAM? First, the B and A sections still exist to speak her language as much as possible, but this time the M section is significantly longer. There is less WD-40, so to speak, and more message. Recalling the boundary guidelines from chapter 3, how did Ron do?

Was Ron clear about the boundary? Yes. She would now be pulled from the specialized work groups and must meet her deadlines by working alone on her projects for the next six weeks.

Was Ron clear about the consequences? Yes. He was clear that if she did not, she would be moved to a different position in a different department. He also was clear that it would involve a demotion of sorts and a salary adjustment down. Finally, note that the consequences would not only be practical and financial, but relational. He spoke her language by noting that she "let the team down" and he was "disappointed."

Did Ron enforce the consequence? He did.

Know when to walk away, know when to run

In this case, enforcing the consequence did mean having to walk away from Andi and demote her only two weeks later. Although Andi lost almost half her wage in the process, the move to a different department ended up being a positive move for all involved. Andi felt bad she let her team down, but the reality was that although she was intellectually capable of doing the job, she found a better fit in her new department. Less was required of her. She always worked in teams, and the level of responsibility fit her better at this point in her journey. Ron also hired someone a little better suited to the needs of his department.

10

The Overanalyzer

"Perfect is the enemy of good"

—Voltaire

Mindset: "Do it right, or don't do it at all. Don't quit until it's perfect."

Behaviors: Over-rehearsing, putting off starting things, inability to quit until "the time is right," working long hours, difficulty completing tasks, and other perfectionistic behaviors

Beliefs: "I must be perfect," "Others are slobs," "The world must have order."

DISC profile: One out of control manifestation of the *C*.

Continuum

Mild	Moderate	Severe
I-----------------------I-----------------------I		
Values detail. Work pace is slower than most, but can complete tasks reasonably	Inability to delegate at times, has difficulty adjusting when redirected	Tedious work style makes task completion almost impossible by deadlines

Description

The Overanalyzer (OA) represents an overdeveloped version of the *C* prototype on the DISC personality profile, and in clinical terms has *obsessive-compulsive* personality traits.

While *D's* and *C's* are both performance oriented, one interesting note is that they fall on opposite ends of the spectrum in terms of evaluating risk. *D's* underestimate (or don't consider it to begin with), while *C's* overestimate danger. Exercising this extreme caution, it can seemingly take forever for the *C* to get things done, while the *D* can impulsively jump into things without having thought them through. In this sense, it sometimes feels like *C's* *overthink* while *D's* "*underthink.*"

When kept in check, these traits seen in the OA that emphasize paying attention to detail can serve companies, organizations, and ministries well. OAs are usually highly intelligent. Their cerebral nature can balance out the intensity of the Bully, the DM, and the LM. There is certainly a role in most industries for people who are analytical, thoughtful, and thorough, and who value quality work. Even for companies that offer products or services that aren't typically associated with those features, every business needs an accountant. And, if it has any online presence, it needs a tech person.

On the downside, people with this style are typically not the most efficient, and they often have difficulty getting things done. This is partially because the "analysis to paralysis" thing influences them to "overthink" and underperform. If something must be absolutely perfect and thought out nine times before taking action, this can certainly slow things down. Also, due to this need to mull things over in their minds before speaking up, the OA's best ideas never actually get shared!

The reality is that everybody has the same 168 hours in every week. However, this type feels like they "never have enough time." Their overanalyzing tendencies keep them from getting desired results because they can't use their time nearly as efficiently as others. "My 168 seems to go a lot faster than everyone else's!" one OA client once told me.

Additionally, people with this style have difficulty delegating due to the fear of something getting done incorrectly. As one of my clients put it, "Others will just screw it up—to maintain an adequate standard I need to do it myself." While they perform the highest quality work, they can also have trouble seeing the bigger picture or vision. It is challenging to understand the scope of the whole forest for people with these traits because they are so intently focusing on one leaf on one branch of one tree. One consequence of this is that it is extremely common for OAs to get lost in focus and completely lose track of time. I had a client one time whose entire shift had ended and he didn't even realize he worked right through lunch!

Another quality in this type is that their need for precision makes it difficult for them to estimate. As an example, our electricity recently went out during a storm. One of my eight-year-old twins, who has a fair amount of **C** in her, said, "Dadda, what time is it?" I told her it was nine o'clock. Once she could get her iPad powered up, she said, "Hey, it's not nine, it's eight fifty-eight!" This quality also shows up in the OA in everyday ways you may not think about. Clients with this mindset have difficulty answering scaling questions. For instance, when I ask most people to rate their stress level on a scale of zero to ten, they may think about it for a second or two, and they throw a number out. The OA, however, may agonize with internal dialogue such as *"Is my level a 6 today or is it a 7? Let me think about answers I have given before and what was going on in my life—I need to convey what I really mean. I have to give an accurate response. What exactly defined a 7 again anyway?"* Supervisors often run into this thought process when asking for an estimate of how a project is coming. "Ballpark figure" and "estimated time frame" are dirty words to the OA.

Overanalyzers are usually "control freaks," but it is important to note that with this personality type it is typically more important to control their *environment* than it is to control people. Some family members of this type would argue vehemently with me on this point. And the fact is that people in their lives are *part of their environment,* so they can end up occupying that role of the object of control; however, as **C**'s who are task oriented, their behaviors serve a different motivation that is not inherently people-driven. Unfortunately, many people in the lives of the OA end up being "collateral damage."

Another way to think about this type of person is that they are an extreme perfectionist. They possess unrealistic standards for themselves and usually for others as well. Even in those people whose mindset only requires perfectionistic behaviors of themselves, the often unattainable goals they set also put undue stress on others. The pressure to meet these self-imposed standards or deadlines can't help but affect those with whom they closely share their lives.

A final part of what this entails relationally is that the hypercritical nature of OAs tends to cause them to miss the good in other people. So that overdeveloped critical part of the mind that naturally looks for the "bad," which serves them well in finding errors nobody else in the company noticed, doesn't serve them as well when pointing out every flaw in loved ones. So, while Bullies don't think about others period, OAs tend to think about them negatively.

Consequently, others often perceive them to be cold, negative, and exhausting to interact with. Their homing in on minute aspects of situations and their related inability to see the big picture can frustrate team members and friends alike.

This personality type also spends a lot of time and energy worrying, and in extreme forms can become quite obsessive. Stress and frustration are the two emotions most frequently experienced by people with this style, which has also been associated with several physical conditions, including headaches, heart disease, weight gain, memory problems, and insomnia just to name a few.

OAs come in all shapes and sizes. One thing every person with this personality type shares, however, is a unique version of the extreme thinking. Middle ground is hard to come by, and it can manifest in part with the following attitudes:

- ♣ "If I am not completely finished, I have to keep working."
- ♣ "Anything less than 100 percent is unacceptable."
- ♣ "Since this proposed solution would only get me 95 percent of what I want, I need to keep arguing."

- ♣ "Just to be sure I have it completely perfectly, I need to go over it again."
- ♣ "To be sure I understand the question perfectly, I need to read it again (and sometimes five times)."
- ♣ "Since she did not say it completely accurately, I need to correct her."
- ♣ "Since she did not clean the house completely right, I need to go back over it."
- ♣ "Since the whole goal was not achieved, it was a complete failure."
- ♣ "Since they don't meet an acceptable standard, others are messy."

You likely believe one or more of the above at least to some degree. Many of us were raised with the mantra "If you can't do something right, don't even do it at all." There is value in taking time to ensure quality. Abraham Lincoln is famous for saying "Give me six hours to chop down a tree and I will spend the first hour sharpening the ax."

As my ACT colleague Marty Antony points out in his book *When Perfect Isn't Good Enough*, perfectionism is a problem that affects people in multiple domains of life. Antony suggests asking the simple question, "Do my high standards help me or hurt me?" Some people use elevated standards in a way that motivates them, which helps promote high achievement. These people get inspired by the words of the legendary football coach Vince Lombardi when he said, "Perfection is not attainable. But if we chase perfection, we find excellence."

However, OAs take this drive for perfection over the top. Due to their extreme rigid thinking, they cannot feel proud of their work if it is merely excellent. If they strive for perfect and achieve excellence it "isn't good enough," so they feel bad about themselves and continue to exhibit extreme behaviors discussed in this chapter that OAs have become notorious for. So for this type we can say that perfect is actually the enemy of excellence.

Red flags

As with traits of each personality style, you can always spot OAs ahead of time if you know what to for. Here are a few red flags to keep an eye out for in different settings.

Overanalyzers red flags in the workplace

- ☐ Did the person take an inordinate amount of time completing the application, references, or prehire information when compared to other applicants?
- ☐ Do they answer interview questions in a slow and deliberate manner, giving far more information, explanation, or detail the question calls for?
- ☐ Ask if they have a history of missing deadlines. Listen for complaints of not having enough time, feeling rushed, or other OA traits blaming others.
- ☐ Have coworkers complained their methodical approach is slowing the team down or frustrating members of the task force?
- ☐ Do they refuse to accept proposals due to only being 98 percent accurate and insist on multiple resubmissions?
- ☐ Do you find them working excessive hours or unauthorized overtime?

- ☐ Is the employee overly critical of coworkers?
- ☐ Do they regularly seem to complain about something?
- ☐ Does their slow, deliberate style keep them from meeting required deadlines?
- ☐ Do they have difficulty negotiating with team members?
- ☐ Do they often blame you or others for "rushing them" and not caring about a job well done?

Overanalyzer red flags in schools

- ☐ Has the student verbalized being bothered by slight imperfections in the classroom, such as a small portion of a line on the board that was omitted when erasing?
- ☐ Do they have difficulty completing timed tests or other class assignments on time?
- ☐ Have you noticed them becoming upset for getting an A– instead of an A (or another excellent score that was less than perfect)?
- ☐ Do they typically demonstrate high-quality work but have difficulty meeting deadlines?
- ☐ Are they overly critical of other students?
- ☐ Do you notice them being overly critical of themselves?
- ☐ Do you notice them getting angry frequently when something in the classroom is not "right" or "the way it should be"?
- ☐ Do you notice a preoccupation with order, details or neatness at their desk or personal space?

Overanalyzer red flags in personal relationships

☐ Do you believe the person sets unrealistic goals for himself or herself?

☐ Do they have high standards for others as well?

☐ Do you notice them becoming controlling or angry when you don't meet a standard you may or may not have agreed to strive for?

☐ Can they experience sustained happiness with life, or do they always seem annoyed with the world?

☐ Do they lack spontaneity in the relationship? Can you surprise them with an impromptu dinner date and they be flexible enough to go? Or must it be "planned" out ahead of time.

☐ Do they regularly run late for family functions, date nights, or other events previously committed to because they "couldn't get away from work" or some other activity?

☐ Do you feel like you often take a back seat to the "project of the moment?"

☐ Does he/she offer frequent criticism or come behind you redoing your work because it didn't quite meet their standards (e.g., cleaning something again just after you did it)?

☐ Do you find them going on and on, and on in conversations to the point that you feel exasperated with them and just want to interrupt by saying "get to the point!"?

A personal example

Sam was an aerospace engineer in his early fifties. He had never been married, though he desperately wanted to be. He sought psychotherapy hoping to receive feedback regarding how he could "find the one."

Sam had several decent guy friends he described as "fairly close" who he hung out with at a local bar every Wednesday night. It became apparent quickly that these friends appeared to often get annoyed with him in response to him talking about his dating life.

Upon getting to know Sam, I discovered he had an active social life. He went out of his way to attend at least one singles group event every weekend in addition to his guys' night on Wednesdays.

I found him to be an extremely genuine, good-hearted guy who had several admirable qualities. He was extremely intelligent, thoughtful, and had a gentle spirit about him. He was a tall, slender man who wore glasses. Although he had been described by some as being "nerdy" he was not terribly unattractive. Sam had dated several women in the past, and as we visited a pattern quickly emerged.

Sam met his first "serious" girlfriend in college. They started dating his senior year and were together a total of eight years. They had several conversations about getting married; however, he said he could not bring himself to do it because she was not quite as intelligent of a person as he had always hoped for and he could not get past the fact that her singing voice was not quite what he had envisioned in a future wife. His next significant relationship was with a tall, attractive woman who worked in a local accounting firm. After five years he decided to end the relationship because while going through some health problems she had put on about ten to fifteen pounds and he no longer found her attractive. A third relationship he described was with a medical student, who, during the ten years they dated, became a surgeon. He loved her "scientific mind" and described their chemistry, including intellectual banter, as stimulating to him. However, in their tenth year of dating when she proposed to him, he told me, "I just couldn't pull the trigger ... I just could not live the rest of my life wondering if I could not have gotten someone a little more attractive."

A workplace example

Boyd worked for a large health-care system in quality control. His department supervisor identified him as a candidate for ongoing coaching as follow up to a leadership development training.

Boyd was a soft-spoken man whose kindness and passion showed through the minute you met him. He possessed a unique combination of strong convictions coupled with a laid-back demeanor. Boyd presented as sharply dressed and well-spoken. While he appeared to go out of his way not to be critical of any of the administrative team, including his supervisor, I could tell he believed what they were asking of him was unfair. "There is just no way it is possible to get everything done," he finally said.

Having worked with many health systems my assumption was that his department was understaffed and had placed unrealistic demands on their employees. However, after speaking with his supervisor as well as others in the department, I concluded that my hypothesis in this particular case was wrong.

As it turned out, it was taking him three times longer than those on his team to assimilate data and run the same reports as everyone else in his work group. He had had three prior meetings with his supervisor with goals of increasing his efficiency, which had been largely unsuccessful. Boyd had also continued to work unauthorized overtime to complete his projects despite repeated directives that it had not been approved in those instances.

When I inquired directly to Boyd regarding these problems, he told me, "Everyone else just rushes through things. Our department isn't called quality control for no reason. There needs to be more quality around here. That's the reason I go over projects three times before I submit them—I just want to be sure they are right."

As we visited, it became clear that not only was his OA qualities causing concern at the office, but it was also creating marital discord as well. "My wife is getting ticked that I keep getting home too late to be a part of the family dinners."

Connecting with the Overanalyzer

Connecting is a foundational element of communicating effectively with anyone. And this truth is only amplified when it comes to dealing with difficult people.

The OA can be difficult to connect with because (1) they aren't inherently "people," and (2) they often annoy others with their picayune responses. Though they can be difficult to connect with in different ways than other types discussed, here are a few tips:

- ❖ **Emphasize shared value of quality**. If they know you value things being done well also, you have scored points with them immediately. Validate problems you have seen with "shortcuts" and frustrations you may have with "careless" and "sloppy" people. Immediately OAs will appreciate it and, to some degree, know you are "one of them."
- ❖ **Communicate the value of preparation**. Alexander Graham Bell once said, "Before anything else, preparation is the key to success." Assure them you believe this, and value preparation over impulsivity.

❖ **Allow ample time**. Preparation takes time, and OAs are deliberate people. Although there will certainly be limits, communicate to them you will make every reasonable effort to give them the time they need to complete their task well.

Top ten tips to disarming the Overanalyzer

1. **Know their triggers and avoid them**. OAs value control. Although some degree of accountability is usually necessary, don't micromanage them. Allow them to work within their comfort zone where they can take charge of the tasks in front of them. Let them be in control of their own world. Allow them to work from home when possible or in isolation for periods of time to accomplish what they need to without being "bothered." Allow minimal socialization. If they don't want to play with the kids on the playground or attend company socials, don't require something that makes them overly uncomfortable.

2. **Feed their need for structure**. OAs thrive on organization. Do everything you can to provide this environment for them. Write on the board what you will cover in class that day. Provide, ahead of time when possible, a written agenda for departmental meetings with items numbered out. Establish and stick to a consistent routine and avoid spontaneous "surprises" when possible.

3. **Anticipate their questions**. It is easy to get annoyed with the OA's barrage of questions. Remember this personality type is overly inquisitive. Be prepared for endless "why" questions. It wouldn't be reasonable to expect a cow not to moo, so don't expect an OA not to question. It's what they do! Finally, it is not

enough to prepare your mindset simply to not be annoyed, so learn to predict what they will ask and prepare credible answers. This style responds well to concrete facts and logic. So do your research. Be prepared with facts or sound rationale. Those who have the gift of gab but provide no meat in their answers will only invite further inquiries from this personality style.

4. **Find ways to utilize their skill sets**. Every setting in life needs organizers. Every corporate environment, classroom, and organization has gifted people who HATE to bother with the details. OAs fantasize about being bogged down in details! Find ways to utilize them in those capacities so the others on the team can be free to use their gifts without having to worry about them.

5. **Keep the main thing the main thing**. Remind them of what the forest looks like. I had a client once who could not understand why his adult daughter refused to go on vacation with him and his wife again. So with his permission I had a conversation with the daughter. She relayed a story in which, on the last vacation to Florida, he refused to pay for milkshakes for her daughters (my client's grand-daughters) because "Why would we pay $6 a piece for a milkshake when we could get one bucket of ice cream and make it ourselves here at the condo?" She reported that when they got in car, he realized they needed gas. However, when he pulled into the filling station, he saw it was $4.69 gallon and stated "we are not paying this much for gas—I saw it for $3.99 on the way in." She then described him going WAY out of the way to find a gas station that had it for $3.99. In doing so, he ran the car out of gas and

had to call AAA. She estimated that it took four hours to get back to his condo from an ice-cream run that should have taken twenty minutes—but he concluded the fiasco by saying—"between getting the ice cream and the other gas we saved a total of $19.79—that's almost $20 we can put toward Disney world tomorrow!" My client was so concerned with the "trees" (in this case financial) that he did not notice the "forest" (that he was damaging his relationships). Remind them of big-picture goals. Whether a relationship with daughter or million-dollar project is at stake—help them focus on what is really important.

6. **Avoid power struggles**. Never argue with someone who must be "right." Don't bicker over details. It will get you nowhere.

7. **Learn to eat sloppy joes**. I had a client one time who said in response to one of our sessions, "I guess I'm just going to have to err on the side of sloppy just to be normal." In a way, this awareness he came to was brilliant. He came to realize that his 80 percent was better than most people's 100 percent. From that moment he began to recognize there were "degrees of excellence." And even though it didn't intuitively feel right to him, his motto became, "do it sloppy." He said he got the image of a sloppy joe in his head. From then on, we jokingly referred to his need to tolerate "sloppy" as a willingness to eat sloppy joes. Slowly but surely, he learned the lesson that if you always wait for the perfect moment or feeling to move forward, not only will you never move forward and grow, but you will likely create many problems in your life along the way.

8. **Shift from problem-focused to solution-focused**. Validate frustration and shift. This style could harp on the problem all day long if you let them. That is only counterproductive. Saying something like this can be helpful: "I know this whole thing has been incredibly frustrating. It is my job to move this forward now. What do you suggest?" Actively shift thinking away from problems and onto potential solutions—even if they don't have a great solution, it shifts their thinking and minimizes negativity spreading throughout the team.

9. **Use timers**. Due to the over-focus element in the thinking style of individuals with this personality style, it can be easy to get "lost in thought" and completely lose track of time. One tip for overcoming this "analysis to paralysis" obstacle is to work with them to set timers or alarms to go off in mutually agreed upon increments. This can help "snap them out of it" and pique their awareness to time. Based on this they can then reset their mindset regarding details, reassess goals and time frames, and push themselves through discomfort to accelerate their pace.

10. **One step at a time**. The old saying is that the best way to eat an elephant is one bite at a time. When a task looks enormous, it is easy for any of us to get overwhelmed. This style gets easily overwhelmed because everything constitutes a "huge task." Break it down for them into small, bite-sized, manageable chunks. This can minimize their "overwhelm," keep things moving, and improve efficiency and productivity.

Speaking their language

Now it is time to communicate strategically. Keeping in mind that communication involves a message sent plus a message received, and that beliefs filter both ends of the interaction, what factors should you consider when preparing your BAM to deal with an OA?

Remember our five questions?

1. Who am I?
2. Who are they?
3. Who are they to me?
4. Who am I to them?
5. How might I need to adapt my natural approach to speak so they will listen. So what would using these as a template to prepare for a conversation actually look like?

Consider an interaction that Boyd's supervisor had with him regarding the ongoing unauthorized overtime. We discussed approaching him prior to the conversation, having him ask himself the following questions:

1. Who am I?

Boyd's supervisor actually had a lot of the *C* trait in him as well—apparently just not nearly as much as Boyd.

2. Who are they?

Boyd, an OA, is obviously an extreme version of the *C*. His need for perfection, precision, and complete assurance of accuracy was the issue at the heart of the problem.

3. Who are they to me?

The supervisor identified that he viewed Boyd as a highly valuable employee, and that he wished many others on the team had the attention to detail. So while he actually related with him and respected him in a number of ways, he grew increasingly frustrated with his continued unauthorized overtime, which now grabbed the attention of the CFO, to whom he was a direct report.

4. Who am I to them?

Upon speaking with him, I figured out that Boyd's supervisor was aware he was becoming mildly annoyed with him, but he did not have any idea the degree to which Boyd viewed his ongoing requests as "unfair."

5. How might I need to adapt my natural approach to speak so they will listen?

Due to my role/relationship with Boyd's supervisor being different than the other examples in this book, in this case we were not able to sit down and map this part out as we did with the other exchanges, although we did discuss the desired approach informally. My educated guess as to how his autopilot style might have come across is as follows:

The Supervisor's Moderate C "Autopilot" Filter	His Sending	Boyd's Filter	His Receiving
"Details are important, but deadlines must be met"	"Boyd—I know you want things to be right—I do too. But I have told your three times that you can't have any more overtime and you keep staying late. You can't punch out late again."	"Things must be perfect."	"He says he wants high quality, but he is still trying to rush me. I don't know how I can ever meet his expectations. He knows what we do. He should get why I need more time."

In this case, because Boyd's supervisor had many similar personality traits, his autopilot delivery did not need significant modifications. We discussed the rationale for adding an extra dose of validation of the *C* traits they had in common and emphasizing shared value, in addition to being careful not to let his annoyance show in his tone of voice. This conversation ensued:

B "Boyd—I appreciate your attention to detail and I respect your passion for maintaining a standard of excellence. I think you know that is important to me as well and frankly I wish more around here were as concerned about quality work as you."

A "It's because I value your thoroughness that I need to have this conversation with you. I know we both care enough about this company to be sure things are done well—and I need to be able to keep you here by my side to ensure that I can have someone who I have confidence in assigning some of these projects to and know will ensure that they are done right."

M "Having said that, I need to be very clear. I have had this conversation with you on two previous occasions. Ralph (the CFO) is now involved, and we cannot have any more unauthorized overtime for any reason. Clock-outs must now never be later than 6:07. The team can also not miss any more deadlines the rest of this calendar year. You know where we are. We have three of these we must be diligent with. He has been very clear with me that I can make no exceptions and that a final notice must be given to those who cannot comply. I'd like for you to take all the time you need, get with Jeff, and work out a plan to ensure you are able to comply. Let me know when you two have been able to work out the details. I will do whatever I can to work with you. Do you have any questions for me?"

What did you notice about this BAM response? There is not any feelings language. It is completely task oriented in nature. Again, this part came naturally to the supervisor, but the conversation intentionally spoke his language in terms of need for quality and respect for high standards. It fed his need for those elements, and then in a very factual and straightforward manner delivered the message.

Setting boundaries and enforcing consequences

Reviewing the guidelines for setting boundaries outlined in chapter 3, how did this talk stack up?

1. Was the supervisor clear about the boundary? Yes. He referenced three different specific deadlines. A specific time frame was given (the end of the calendar year.) Expectations were laid out in precise numbers. ZERO more hours of overtime would be allowed and 6:07 was the latest time anyone would be permitted to clock out.

2. Was Boyd's supervisor clear about the consequences? Yes. "Final notice" would be given if he overstepped the boundaries. No lines could be crossed if he wanted to maintain his employment with the organization.

3. Were the consequences enforced? Thankfully, in this case, he did not need to enforce them. We came up with a detailed plan to help Boyd develop a specific schedule for operating by. It helped him identify what time increments he had to accomplish certain portions of given tasks. We also worked to help him increase his awareness as to when those periods had elapsed and put safeguards in place to ensure he knew when he needed to move on. The final difficult task, which he did demonstrate some improvement on, was being OK with "good enough" and recognizing his standard for completeness was different than others. We continued to emphasize relational and occupational consequences awaiting him if he failed to lower his standards, become more efficient, and at times leave something "incomplete."

Know when to walk away, know when to run

I have no doubt that if Boyd failed to make the required changes, he would have lost his job, and perhaps his marriage. His supervisor was not only personally annoyed but was under pressure from the executive team. Thankfully, Boyd made enough changes to keep his job. But I have worked with many OAs who have not made the necessary changes. If you are dealing with an OA who cannot accept anything less than perfect, it might be time to move on. In Sam's case, although he ultimately ended the three relationships alluded to above, he later had a relationship ended by his girlfriend due to his overly critical nature. She decided she could not live the rest of her life under a microscope for every imperfection. There is a point that if people with these traits cannot lower their standards, cut themselves some slack, or give others a little grace, that life in your arena may be better off without them.

11

The Skeptic

"Trust, but verify."

—Russian proverb, Ronald Regan

Mindset: "Others are untrustworthy. You can never be sure what people are up to."

Behaviors: Relentless questioning, hesitating, double-checking, withholding information

Beliefs: "I might get taken advantage of."

DISC profile: One out of control manifestation of the *C*.

Continuum

Mild	Moderate	Severe
I----------------------I		I
Mild skepticism, Quiet, not voluntarily forthcoming	questions, badgers, constantly checking what they are told	Paranoia, complete Mistrust, agitation or Aggression when feels threatened

Description

The Skeptic represents an overdeveloped version of the *C* prototype on the DISC profile, and in clinical terms, often has traits of a *paranoid* personality. It is important to note that many people have some of these traits who are not fully diagnosable. In general, the person with this type of personality typically just strikes you as always a little bit *suspicious*.

When kept in check, these traits make for good protectors. Since they are always on guard for potential threats, they can be extremely valuable in contexts where you or your entity faces actual malevolent intent. These traits serve a person well in roles such as FBI, CIA, other law enforcement, security agents, defense attorneys, and other protective roles. If an outside force really is trying to take advantage of you in some way, you don't want to put a gullible person in charge. Also on the upside, if you can earn the trust of a Skeptic, you have a friend for life. Once you finally earn that coveted place of trust, they can be fiercely loyal.

On the downside, their lack of trust, when unwarranted, can cause problems in relationships, ministry work, community service, or any context where trust and teamwork are necessary. Skeptics value control, so they usually come across as "take charge" people; however, deep down they have many insecurities. Skeptics assume you always mean them harm in some way, so they constantly and vigilantly look for signs of maltreatment or ulterior motives. They don't trust what you say. They double-check what you do. They often won't share with you what they are up to for fear that you might use it against them. Finally, if you do wrong them, they will remember it—forever! Remember, since they expected you to do them wrong in the classroom or on the corporate ladder, once they have "evidence" you did, they will hold onto it. Skeptics are excessively unforgiving.

Some examples of Skeptic attitudes include:

- ♣ "Because you have authority over me, you will use it in some way to hurt me."
- ♣ "If I give you any personal information, you will use it in some way to hurt me."
- ♣ "Since you are under me on the totem pole, I have to watch my back or you will pass me up."
- ♣ "If I intimidate you, you won't try to come at me."
- ♣ "If I don't share what I am up to, others can't use it against me."
- ♣ "If we upset the waitress, she may put something in our food."

Finally, Skeptics then may seek out the companionship of others who share similar themes in beliefs related to "cover-ups," "foul play," or "tampering." Research also suggests that rates of people joining groups holding to conspiracy theories related to UFOs, deaths and disappearances, and business tampering are on the rise.

Red flags

As with traits of each personality style, you can always spot Skeptics ahead of time if you know what to look for. Here are a few red flags to keep an eye out for in different settings.

Skeptic red flags in the workplace

- ☐ Do they have bad things to say about previous employment experiences?
- ☐ Do they have a history of being involved with lawsuits, grievances or other punitive efforts against previous employees or coworkers?
- ☐ Are they reluctant to provide routine personal information for necessary paperwork?
- ☐ If they have a history of previous complaints lodged, ask about them.
- ☐ Do they use conspiracy-related language as they talk about previous work environments?
- ☐ Do they verbalize past or present beliefs that a person was "out to get them"?

Skeptic red flags in schools

- ☐ Are they "loners" or frequently seen withdrawing from other teachers or students?
- ☐ Do they pick and choose the information they share with you carefully?

- ☐ Do they flat out refuse to answer questions when asked?
- ☐ Do they get irritated or agitated when asked to reveal personal information?
- ☐ Do you see them looking over their shoulder or watching their backs?
- ☐ Do they keep their distance from other children at recess or on the playground?

Skeptic red flags in personal relationships

- ☐ Do they take relatively lengthy periods of time to disclose surface-level personal information? (Where they work, what their children's names are, etc.)
- ☐ Do they dodge, change the subject, or otherwise avoid when you ask questions about them?
- ☐ Do they make accusations of unfaithfulness even after you have been dating/married for an extended time when there has been no history of infidelity?
- ☐ Have they become controlling about who you spend your time with? Demanding that you spend no time with people outside of your relationship?
- ☐ Do they badger you with phone calls, texts, or DMs when out of their sight?

A personal example

Jerry, a single man in his late thirties, sought me out for assistance with his anxiety. When I asked him what kinds of things made him anxious, he replied, "Mainly people."

I asked him what type of people made him the most anxious, and he said, "Pretty much all people." I asked him if highly successful people made him more anxious than less successful people. He said, "Not really." Then I was curious if being in the presence of women made him more anxious than being in the presence of men. "Nah." I then asked if there was a particular activity such as giving a class presentation or being at a party that made him more anxious than other situations. "They are all just as bad," he said.

My search to narrow down a more specific trigger was officially going poorly.

I finally countered with a different type of question that was more fruitful. "What is it about people I asked about that makes you so anxious—what are you concerned about most?"

"You just can't ever be sure people are shooting straight with you," he responded.

It became apparent pretty quickly that Jerry had a general mindset that told him "People are out to get you."

Further conversation revealed he was suspicious of classmates, friends, coworkers, and previous girlfriends. He had actually just been engaged in a verbal altercation (that almost got physical) with one of his two friends because "I saw the way he looked at my girl while we were shooting pool. I know I've only taken her out twice but he's a player and I saw the look in his eye when he saw her sitting in the corner."

A workplace example

Following a soft skills communication-based training, Debbie's manager identified her as one of the people on their team who could benefit from ongoing one-to-one work with a corporate coach. She had held the same job with her company for the past eight years, but she believed she was now on thin ice.

According to her manager, she had become increasingly challenging for the team to work with and recently was the target of a hostile work environment complaint filed with HR.

Debbie acknowledged that she had become increasingly disgruntled over the years and was convinced that now, more than ever, members of her team were "stealing her ideas" and presenting them to their direct supervisor as their own.

In response to this, she had essentially shut down, stopped contributing to her work group, and spent more time going to the break room (which could only be accessed by walking by the supervisor's office) as she was "curious who might be in there talking to her."

Her peers encouraged her to contribute more and affirmed some of her past ideas. Debbie could not receive this because "They are only asking me to share more because they just want to steal and take credit for more of my ideas." Her direct supervisor had attempted to give her positive feedback, and asked her to work on a different project where her ideas could be "her own" but she refused to switch groups because "if I take the transfer they will just document it and use it as evidence that I can't play well with others."

It came to light in the first session that she had been let go from her previous job eight years ago for getting combative with her supervisor. "He was trying to set me up so I would get written up—that's why I didn't do what he told me to."

Connecting with the Skeptic

Connecting is a foundational element of communicating effectively with anyone. And this truth is only amplified when it comes to dealing with difficult people. And of the difficult personality types, the Skeptic may be the most difficult to connect with. It is important to remember that even though they likely won't trust you to the degree others might, it is still possible to develop some, even if shallower, level of connection. Here are a few tips:

- ❖ **Validate their skepticism**. It is true that not all people are trustworthy. Colleagues do stab us in the back. Students do target other students. Let them know you are aware this happens and commend them for being onto this and having more discernment than most.
- ❖ **Story time!** Tell a story about a time somebody pulled one over on you—and how you or others got hurt as a result. This communicates to them that you understand, to some degree, on a personal level. Convey to them that you have seen or experienced the dangers on a playground or peril that came come from trusting the wrong people in the workplace or how you have been hurt by the church.
- ❖ **Accept their mistrust**. Emphasize that you are not expecting them to trust or believe everyone. That would be unwise and perhaps even unsafe. Reinforce that they certainly don't need to trust everyone and that it can be wise not to accept everything at face value. Rather, stress to them that it is important to determine who can be trusted and who cannot, and what is necessary to move forward in their role to do what is required of them.

Top ten tips for disarming a Skeptic

1. **Know their triggers and avoid them**. Remember, the Skeptic becomes especially vigilant in situations where they need to be vulnerable. It is also important to understand their concept of vulnerability likely differs from yours. To the degree you can,

accommodate requests in this regard. For instance, be willing to email something at their request so they "have documentation" even in situations you ordinarily would not. Allow minimal socialization. If there is no need for them to go to the outside office party, give them permission to stay home if the idea makes them uncomfortable.

2. **Use your patience!** This phrase I use with my small twins doubles as great advice for anyone dealing with a Skeptic. It can be easy to get impatient when interacting with this personality type. Answer as many questions as they have. If you get annoyed, they will see it and read something into it far worse than you were really thinking.

3. **Feed their need for security**. Tell them they can come and go from a church service as they please. Allow them to sit in the corner with nobody behind them in the classroom. And go a little further with the trait if you can. Don't only attempt to minimize their skepticism. Look for ways to harness it in useful ways. Put them in charge of company security or have them be the watchmen on the playground.

4. **Be transparent**. What is appropriate may vary according to context and the role you have in this person's life. But the more open you are with them the more they are likely to drop their guard, even if slightly and open up a bit to you. While psychotherapists and coaches are notorious for having poor boundaries (e.g., sharing too much personal information and for the wrong reasons), a surprising number also err on the other side putting up a stoic veneer of invulnerability and refuse to share anything. Sidenote: If you have a therapist who answers your question with a question—run! There

is a middle ground that is appropriate for different people and in different situations. But even in my role as a therapist I was more transparent with this style than most—and there is no doubt it contributed to effective outcomes.

5. **Be prepared for questions**. Dogs bark, the sun sets, cows moo, and Skeptics ask questions. While many managers, teachers, and peers get exceedingly frustrated with this, the culprit is largely a product of *your* thinking if you let it affect you! We discussed expectations at the outset. Revisit the opening chapters if you need to. But it is completely irrational for us to expect people to behave in ways that go against their character or established patterns of behavior.

6. **Pose possibilities**. Offer them alternative explanations they might not have thought about on their own. This can be sticky, and must be approached with care, but can make or break who can work with a Skeptic and who cannot. Validate that "You may very well be right, but did you ever consider that when she made the comment, she could have been referring to such and such?" These will often be met immediately with resistance, but as you develop rapport with them as well as establish a history of generating successful ideas, they can open themselves up more to your suggestions over time.

7. **Drop the rope**. There are two ways to win a tug-of-war. If they fail to see any merit in your alternative explanations, don't perpetuate the fight. Resist the urge to defend yourself—unless absolutely necessary for practical reasons (e.g., supervisor believes what is being said and not speaking up could cost you a promotion, etc.). Avoid argumentation. This tactic is crucial for managing mistrust. A version of

this was mentioned in connecting, and it can be a helpful ongoing tactic as well. Accept their skepticism so long as it does not interfere with necessary task completion. If they ask for something in writing you normally would never put in writing but there is no harm in doing so, take the time to do it for them. Don't take it personally that they don't trust you and allow it to push your buttons. Teachers sometimes invite power struggles trying to get a student to trust them when it is not necessary and create blowups that did not need to occur. The minute you argue with a Skeptic, you have already lost.

8. **Agree to disagree.** Don't get in the power struggle, but also don't stay you agree with something you don't. Politely make it OK to differ in opinions. Foster a culture where all opinions hold value and disagreements become opportunities for growth. When various viewpoints are normalized by the workplace or classroom, it can be more acceptable for the Skeptic to walk away without escalating.

9. **Search for solutions.** While having these conversations, remain solution-focused. Skeptics often get hell-bent on remaining focused on the triggering event and may even be punitive. Validate, and ask them to be on your team moving forward. "I don't blame you for being upset over that—it was a pretty big deal—as the manager I need to move this forward now and I'd love your input regarding where to go from here. What do you suggest?" Constantly elicit their input by reframing using solution-oriented language: "I have certainly heard you—where would you advise we go from here?" This sends the message without actually saying it—"It is time to move on!"

10. **Point out consequences of suspiciousness/skepticism.** As consequences arise, point them out at appropriate times. Be particularly observant of skeptical behaviors creating problems that are counterproductive to *their* goals and desires.

Speak their language

Now it is time to communicate strategically. Keeping in mind that communication involves a message sent plus a message received, and that beliefs filter both ends of the interaction, what factors would/should you consider when preparing your BAM to deal with a Skeptic?

Remember our five questions?

1. Who am I?
2. Who are they?
3. Who are they to me?
4. Who am I to them?
5. How might I need to adapt my natural approach to speak so they will listen?

So what would using these as a template to prepare for a conversation with a Skeptic actually look like?

Consider the following example from an interaction between Debbie, her newly appointed supervisor Charmaine, and the HR director—around the hostile work environment complaint. In preparation, she asked herself the following questions:

1. Who am I?

A brief preliminary chat revealed Charmaine had strong *S* traits in her personality.

2. Who are they?

We had already identified Debbie as a Skeptic. She had out of control *C* traits sprinkled in with a fair amount of *D*. This tended to manifest in making her quick to anger, highly punitive, and excessively unforgiving.

3. Who are they to me?

Charmaine viewed Debbie as volatile, explosive, and punitive—a ticking time bomb just waiting to explode. While her perception was fairly accurate, the strong people-pleasing qualities in Charmaine's personality probably caused her to overestimate the "harshness" Debbie exhibited. Interviewing witnesses to this event in question helped calm her nerves a bit. Nevertheless, given the interplay of types of personality traits present in these two, this was destined to be a tense conversation.

4. Who am I to them?

Though Charmaine was not new to the company, she believed Debbie viewed her as the new kid on the block because she was the newly appointed supervisor in that department. She thought Debbie also considered her a naive person who would believe any and all allegations conjured up against her and was out to get her. On this perception, she was pretty much dead on.

5. How might I need to adapt my natural approach to speak so they will listen?

Asking the question, "If my autopilot goes unchallenged, how would I likely send the message and how would he likely receive it?" Charmaine and I predicted it would look like this:

Charmaine's S "Autopilot" Filter	Her Sending	Debbie's Filter	Her Receiving
"Keep the peace"	"I am really sorry to have to have this conversation. Somebody filed a complaint against you and I don't like it at all. I want both of you to be OK and be able to get along."	"Others can't be trusted."	"She is just saying that. She doesn't want me to be OK. She doesn't understand how cutthroat it is in this department. She doesn't know anything and I can't believe a word she says."

In this case, Charmaine's autopilot would need to be reprogrammed significantly. We coached Charmaine on how to compensate for her natural tendencies as well as how to speak Debbie's language. The BAM conversation, which was a little more complex than previous examples, occurred as follows:

B "Debbie, thank you for coming in today. I don't blame you for being a little guarded with me since I called you in on such short notice. Let me just start by telling you I personally hate to deal with these hostile work environment complaints. So many of them are frivolous and unwarranted and so many people are just out to get others back these days. I know that even though I am the supervisor I am the newbie in the department and so it is understandable that people don't trust me yet ... that's why they made Val (HR) sit in with me ... nobody has reason to trust me yet. (laughing a bit)."

A "I want you to know that even though it may not feel that way now—and I understand that it does not for some people—this is a safe company to work for—and I want you to know that even though somebody was upset with you, that your position with this company is safe as well. Although I have not been here to see it, Val has conveyed your history here and I know you have given eight years of quality service to our mission. The reason I have to have this conversation with you is to be sure this workplace environment continues to feel like a safe place for everyone."

M "Because the complaint was filed, we do have to discuss this. I wanted to let you know that I talked with members of the team who were present when this happened. And although they all said your voice was a little loud and perhaps a bit harsh, which does need to change, not a single one of them felt threatened by you or believed you had any dangerous intentions. I see from your written response to the allegations that when you raised your voice at Shaniqua and she accused you of yelling at her, you were feeling threatened ... Can you tell me a little more about that?"

Debbie responds in a defensive and blaming, yet controlled manner. "Yes, I have had my work stolen here before, and the way she was talking I didn't know what she was up to. Fred and Kari were there too, and I didn't know if they were in on it or not also. So I was feeling a little ganged up on."

Charmaine resumes continuing to use the BAM approach.

B "It sounds like in that moment you really sensed a real danger that you might lose your position and you saw her as a target of that threat. I can assure you that is not the case.

I will even share with you that when I feel threatened, the hair on the back of my neck just sort of automatically stands up like a cat. So I know what it is like to feel on the defensive. I know you did not mean any harm."

M "But in order for me to protect you against these types of claims in the future I need you to not raise your voice or yell at anybody moving forward anywhere on the property—can I have your word on this? If so, I will ask you to sign acknowledging that we had this conversation and this will be over."

Debbie is subdued, and quietly responds with "What does this signature mean?"

"Your signature protects me. I don't have to tell you how people can be vengeful so I need you to you have my back by signing this. It documents that I have done my job, that we have had this conversation, that no claims were substantiated against you, and that we have an agreement moving forward. I will also then be willing to work with you to see what we can do to make sure you know that your ideas and contributions are protected and that ultimately your security is insured."

What did you notice about this BAM response? Since things were tense from the outset, it got straight to the point, giving Debbie no additional time to misinterpret others' intent and escalate. It carried heavy doses of **B** around validating her mindset of mistrust. In this conversation, Charmaine immediately attempts to disarm Debbie's defenses by validating her guardedness but doing so by assigning an alternative meaning to it ("because I called you in here on short notice"). We had talked this over thoroughly, and Charmaine knows the "short notice" has nothing to do with it—that Debbie would be on guard regardless of the notice. But by assigning a common meaning to it, she normalizes Debbie's presentation from the get-go, providing a slightly more open door to broach the issue through. An additional feature of this BAM is that it illustrates that at times, you must double down and continue to validate the belief (**B**) before proceeding with additional statements or requests (**M**s).

Setting boundaries and enforcing consequences

Are boundaries and consequences set in the interaction above? Let's look, using the guidelines from chapter three.

1. **Is Charmaine clear about a boundary?** In the above example, a boundary is mentioned and a line of sorts is drawn "I need you not to yell at anybody moving forward."
2. **Is Charmaine clear about the consequences?** No. They are not even mentioned. But this is again purposeful at this point in the life of the problem given the type of HC person involved. We know any mention of consequences now will be perceived as a threat by Debbie through her filters and any hope of rapport being built between the new supervisor and her employee will be dead on arrival. The goal of this conversation is primarily to build some, even if minor, connection to a potentially problematic employee while mentioning that some behavior change is needed in a nonthreatening way.
3. **Did Charmaine follow through?** It is not possible to follow through with consequences that were never set. Due to the timing of this specific integration, Charmaine handled this as well as she could have. If additional conversations need to happen in the

future, write-ups, performance improvement plans, and eventually termination of employment may be on the table as potential consequences.

Know when to walk away, know when to run

Termination is the final of the potential consequences, and this will certainly be a possibility down the road for Debbie if she does not demonstrate the ability to change some of her work behaviors. Whether you are looking at termination of employment, ending a relationship, or expelling a student from school, "termination" steps always constitute a last resort. And unlike some types of HC people, such as the Bully who can benefit from hearing the potential future consequences, the Skeptic perceives consequences as threats and it is counterproductive to share them this soon in the process.

Some research suggests that Skeptics are the least likely of all the HC personalities to make meaningful change. Because of this, "walking away" in some form ends up being a more common outcome with this style than with others. This obviously reinforces their beliefs that others can't be trusted—but this is my concern as a therapist or coach, not yours as someone in their personal life. For human beings who wish the best for our fellow man, sometimes this is hard to see. But insight and change are the task of each individual person him or herself, and not the job of the teacher, employer, or loved one.

12

Disarming My Difficult People

ere is where the rubber meets the road! Now that you are armed with all the knowledge you need to deal with the difficult people in your life, it is time for you to apply it! Henry Ford (among others) is attributed with debunking the "knowledge is power" myth and emphasizing the idea that knowledge is essentially useless if not organized and intelligently directed through specific plans of action. This chapter will help you spell out your specific plan of action.

The initial step is to examine the relationships in your life. While there are many ways you can do this, I am going to walk you through a model I adapted from Prochaska and DiClemente's stages of change work that has resonated deeply with my clients over the past twenty years.

First spend a few minutes identifying all the significant people (whether you like them or not) in your life in this current season. Anyone you still have regular contact with or has some influence over your emotions should be included. Place them in the set of concentric circles below in terms of how close you perceive your relationship. Those who enjoy a good "play on words" to help them remember concepts may benefit from thinking of these *intimacy circles* in terms of the phrase "into-me-see." That is, when evaluating your relationships and considering what circle to put people in ask yourself the question, "How much do I let this person 'see into me?'"

People whom you allow to see into you 100 percent would go in circle number 1. Another way to think about this might be to say that if you had a problem in any area of life, no matter how personal, you would be able to share it with that person. If they meet this criteria, they likely belong in your innermost circle.

Perhaps you then have people you are mostly open with; however, you may have an area or two of your life that is just a little too personal to go there with—these individuals would be candidates for circle number 2. People in circle number 3 then are folks you may be comfortable with or willing to share about half of your personal life with. Circle number 4 typically consists of casual acquaintances. They may know you are married, but no details about your spouse or the dynamic of your relationship. They may know where you are from, but no specifics about your family of origin or personal background. Or they could know where are employed, but nothing of the nature of work that you do.

And finally there is circle number 5. These people get nothing. They may be individuals you just met—so perhaps they could be candidates to move closer into your circles in the future—but at this point you are not comfortable sharing much of anything with them. Or, and more often this is the case, they could be individuals who at one point held a closer or more intimate place in your life, but did something to violate your trust, so you had to "boot them out" a rung or two or five! Estranged family members you still see a time or two a year, exes with whom you share children so still have to interact with, and those with whom you sit on a board with or work at your company you have no respect for are examples of people commonly occupying the highly coveted circle number 5.

So take all the time that you need. Make a list of the current characters in the drama that is your life, carefully consider what circle accurately represents your current relationship with them (how it currently realistically *is*, not how you would like it to be), and write their name in the appropriate circle.

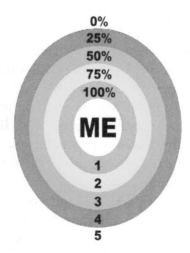

Once you have examined your relationships, reflect on the following questions.

- ᨆ What general observations do I make when I look at my circles?
- ᨆ What themes do I notice in my relationships?

- What do I like about my circles?
- In what way(s) could my circles be "unhealthy?"
- What changes would I like to make to my circles?
- If I revisited this exercise again a year from now, how would I like them to be different?
- What specific steps could I take to influence my circles in positive ways?

Keep in mind, possible goals for circles might include:

Identifying new people to add to your circles. Some people make the general observation that they don't have enough people period in their circles. Others have done the tough work of moving unhealthy people out but now that they don't have unhealthy people, they have no people! Some people have plenty of people in their circles, but nobody in circle number 1 and no candidates in their outer four circles for that precious place in their lives. These are some scenarios in which you may want to start by simply making of qualities of the people you want in your life. Follow that by brainstorming a list of places where you could meet people with those attributes. Then start making some inquiries.

Moving people closer in your circles. Perhaps you have not trusted anyone fully, see the need to grow in this area, and don't know where to start. If you have no friends in your inner circles and no candidates in your outer circles to consider moving in, consult the action step above. But if you have people in your circles 2 to 5 who could be the types of people you want closer in your life, your next step is not to try to find new people but to start to assess the trustworthiness of the people you already have! Take small steps. Invite someone to coffee. Set up a Zoom call. Share one small piece of personal information you had previously been unwilling to share. See how they handle it. If they are trustworthy with one small piece, give them a second. Continue to evaluate. If they are not, go back to the drawing board. Hire a coach or therapist to help you work this process if you don't trust your judgment or need help.

Moving unhealthy people OUT one or more circles. This may be the most common goal for people doing "circle work." Monitoring how much you share with people, how much time you spend interacting with people, and the health and character of the persons you are spending the most time with. Set boundaries. Enforce them. Set them again. Enforce them again. Reteach people how to treat you. Oh, and many of you will need to end harmful relationships completely moving people all the way to circle 5.

Keeping people right where they are at. This option never crosses the mind of some. Perhaps you are happy having your mother in circle number 2, but you have to be the one to reach out with some regularity to schedule that monthly get-together required to maintain circle 2 closeness. Or maybe you are fine having that occasionally obnoxious friend Gary in circle 3—you just don't want him any closer! He may be great to grab a drink with or catch a big game with, but you can only stand him in small doses. Maybe Jill is a bit of a gossip, but she provides intellectual stimulation in the reading club and is fun at the monthly bunco game. Just because she may be banging your door down to get closer in doesn't mean you have to let her in closer or eliminate her from the position she currently holds in your life if you enjoy where she's at.

Intentionally managing responses to people in our circles. Finally, some relationships we might prefer to end, but cannot completely due to circumstances out of our control (the pompous dude you can't stand who married your big sister). We teach people how to treat us—and we do this essentially by what we say yes to and what we say no to. One of the best pieces of wisdom I learned in graduate school from the great family systems legends was the idea that "you cannot not communicate." The reality is that we send people messages reinforcing how to treat us by every action and inaction we choose—and often outside of our awareness. Think about what messages are being communicated when:

- The high *S* employee says yes every time the manager makes a request to work unpaid overtime to "help out the team"
- The father bales his teenager out shielding him from consequences every time he gets in trouble at school
- The mother who ignores her child begging for her affection at the swimming pool because her attention is glued to her device
- The supervisor who portrays outward annoyance every time an employee has a question
- The church or nonprofit organization that continually offers assistance with no requirements to individuals fully capable providing for themselves
- The teacher who devotes all their attention to students who act out and ignores those who quietly comply doing the right thing every day.

The list of possible scenarios is endless. Identify what applies to your life and your situations. Be cognizant of what you communicate and the messages you send by your responses (and lack of responses). Increase your awareness of the dynamics with those in your circles and even if you can't end certain relationships completely, learn to handle them more skillfully.

Whether you have difficult people in your life or not, this has proven to be a powerful exercise for each of us to complete at least once. And if you value personal development and enjoy seeing growth play out in the context of your relationships, I recommend you do revisit it annually.

Dealing with my difficult people

Now that you are equipped with the primary tool we use for helping people do relationship work, let's help you apply this to the difficult person/people in YOUR life.

First, make a list of the difficult people you have identified in your circles. For each, ask yourself the following:

- ✒ What circle are they in?
- ✒ What circle would I like them to be in?
- ✒ What role do they play in my life?
- ✒ How important is it that I move them?
- ✒ How could it affect me or others if I don't move them?

If you decide you need to initiate some change with that person, use the following worksheet to guide you through your application of the process laid out in this book.

The potential "difficult" person in my life I am dealing with is _____

My relationship to him/her is _____

I would put them in the following category of difficult people _____

Red flags I have observed in them include:
1.
2.
3.

I have seen them play out in the following interactions

_____

_____

_____

I will use the following connecting strategies with them:
1.
2.
3.

Tips I will use when interacting with him/her include:
1.
2.
3.

I will structure my BAM communication with them as follows.

_____

_____

_____

_____

_____

_____

_____

_____

_____

I could envision having to set the following boundaries with him/her:

1.

2.

3.

I am willing to follow through the following consequences with him/her:

1.

2.

3.

I will know it is time to walk away from this person/ situation when:

_____

_____

_____

My action plan for today is ...

If it doesn't work, I will ...

If I still need help, I will reach out to the following friends or professionals

1.

2.

3.

13

The Bright Side

Perhaps your mother told you "If you can't say anything nice, don't say anything at all." Obviously, I disagree with your mother. I have said a lot of not-so-nice things about each type of difficult person. But it's because I wrote this book for you, not for them. And not for your mother. I wanted you to know how to handle a variety of types of HC individuals when you encounter them in your lives. I wanted you to have the skills to recognize them and deal with them differently, so they no longer have the ability to drive you nuts. For these reasons it was necessary to highlight problem behaviors and ways of interacting.

I believe many strength-based proponents have taken the "no judgment zone" a bit too far. We must make judgments to exercise the discernment that is sorely missing in so many relationships today.

However, I also believe the role of strengths-based work is important. I agree with the many who think its role has been underutilized in psychology until more recent years. Although when dealing with HC personalities, simply developing and harnessing strengths alone is not enough, it can play a vital role that should not be ignored.

Thus this book has focused on how to deal with people whose out of control traits can harm others. Now that we have done that, I wanted to close by stressing that even people with these HC personality types have strengths.

I taught my twins as early as age six (raise your hand if you would hate having a certified cognitive therapist as a parent) when something bad had happened to ask, "What's the bright side?" We even made a game of it. When one of the three of us was talking about something "bad" one of us would yell "BRIGHT SIDE!" and the person had to stop (talking) in their tracks, think for a moment, and identify how, even if in a small way, the event offered some silver lining. This didn't mean we ignored the bad. We never did. But it helped create a way to acknowledge the "bad" so it could be dealt with, but also not be consumed with it, and to learn to focus on some aspect of good. I've heard it said that optimists are wrong just as much as a pessimist—but they have a lot more fun!

When dealing with difficult people, it can be easy to get consumed with the bad. Because there is so much of it. And because those are the traits that drive *us* nuts! So we will end this book by helping you look at the bright side. This can help us cultivate empathy, create levity in tense situations, and sometimes shift the dynamic, even if not ideal, to a more tolerable one. The graphic below offers strengths for us to focus on—if nothing else to remind ourselves—that each of these people who have made our lives so miserable in some way also has good in them.

The Bully	The Con Artist
• Assertive • Decisive • Direct • Determined • Resilient • Productive	• Daring • Does what it takes to accomplish objective • Calm under pressure • Willing to take risks • Charming • Clever
The Drama Mamma	**The Victim**
• Spontaneous • Enthusiastic • Fun • Stimulating • Strong verbal communicators • Presents well / concerned with image • Energetic	• Acknowledges problems • Doesn't sweep issues under rug • Sympathizes with pain • Calls out abuse of power • Gets seriousness of situations • Advocates for workplace fairness
The Land Mine	**The Yes Man/Ma'am**
• Passionate • Supportive • Brings the energy! • Advocates for others • Creative • Intelligent	• Supportive • Reliable • Steady • Consistent • Concerned with others feelings • Approachable/warm
The Overanalyzer	**The Skeptic**
• Organized • Catches mistakes others don't • High-quality work • Outcome oriented • Detail oriented • Thoughtful before acting • Intelligent • Analytical/technical	• Asks the tough questions • Protects • Sees outside threats before others • Devoted • Loyal • Persistent

A concluding tip. When it is hard to see good in someone who drives you nuts, remember each DISC style shares something in common with two of the other three styles, and sometimes it can be helpful for our frustration tolerance to focus on those.

For instance, if you have a lot of *D* features in your personality and a DM or Victim is annoying you, you can remind yourself that at least you share outgoing traits with them. And, if you are being rubbed the wrong way by a Skeptic or an OA, sometimes it can be helpful to remember they value task completion just as much as you do and they don't waste time socializing like those other slackers!

If your primary style is *I*, and you are experiencing an LM or a YM as difficult, it may help your mindset to focus on how important people are to them as well. Or, if you are having conflict with a Bully or a Con Artist, you may benefit from remembering they are outgoing and direct as well.

On the other hand, if your personality is high in *S* traits, and you are upset with a DM or Victim, you may want to remind yourself that even though you don't like how they show it, people's feelings are super important to them also. If your difficult person is an OA, perhaps a shift in your thinking may help you appreciate their reserved nature compared to someone who always creates chaos.

Finally, if you have strong *C* features in your personality and a Bully rushes you, it can be helpful to remember that even though you don't appreciate their specific behaviors in the moment, their ultimate goal is the same as yours: project completion. If a YM annoys you wanting to talk forever, you may benefit from focusing on their reserved nature you share with them.

To put this all together, you can start by recognizing and dealing intentionally with problematic behavior in your setting. Act strategically and swiftly. Don't make excuses for them or come up with reasons to avoid it. Set boundaries and walk away from the relationship if need be. But as you are doing all of this, focus on strengths as much as you can. View them as fellow human beings who are genuinely hurting and have no better ways to express it. Seeing the "bright side" in them will restore your internal peace and help you communicate with them in more compassionate ways as you do what you need to do.

*For a deeper dive into strengths- based work in corporate settings, I highly recommend Kieran Patrick at kpc@kieranpartick.com

CONCLUSION

Awareness and Application

Awareness

Following my 2018 speaking tour in South Africa as I boarded the flight from Cape Town to Paris, a flight attendant made the following announcement:

> *"Ladies and gentlemen ... If you would each be so kind as to look in the aisle in front of you and then behind you—if you notice that there is nobody in front of you and then you turn around and see that there is a line of thirty people behind you, this means that it is indeed YOU that is the one holding up the line. If you make this observation kindly exit the aisle as quickly as possible so we can minimize our already late departure."*

I love awareness. And subtlety!

While this was a humorous and nonthreatening way to make a point, the reality is that we all have our blind spots—parts of our personalities that others see more accurately than we do. As I mentioned in chapter 2, this is one of the things that makes difficult people difficult. But HC individuals aren't the only ones with blind spots. We all have them. Though hopefully most of ours are smaller spots rather than gaping holes.

Humans in general have notoriously poor self-awareness. A survey many years ago, I believe in *The New York Times* (I was unable to retrieve it prior to this publication), revealed that 90 percent of people surveyed believed that they were in the top 10 percent of drivers. So there are all these bad drivers out there causing havoc on the roads ... but it is always somebody else! The reality is that all of us, to varying degrees, have distorted perceptions regarding ourselves and our abilities.

Nobody realizes growing up that their home environment is unhealthy. How would they? It's all they knew. When we don't have complex thinking and the ability to make an observational comparison, we can't recognize something as "off." Developing this awareness is trickier than it sounds. I have a friend, who in this way is a microcosm of society, that one evening at dinner proudly claims, "one of my strengths is that I am extremely self-aware." He says this *during* a conversation in which he rubs two other friends of ours the wrong way who did not talk to him for months after that night in the sports bar! Likely anyone who self-proclaims to have great awareness inherently lacks it.

Socrates is often credited with saying "The unexamined life is not worth living." While this seems a bit extreme, it is fair to say the unexamined life makes living a meaningful life more difficult. My buddy has no idea what he said that ran two friends off, and now is less happy because of it. Sadly, millions of people worldwide do this regularly.

When I do my daily Facebook discussion questions, posts that ask for advice have 66 percent more engagement than posts asking for personal reflection. As Leo Tolstoy once famously said, "Everyone wants to be part of the solution, few people see their role in the problem. "Why? Because it is easier for most to point out others' shortcomings than to recognize and be vulnerable about our own.

One key area (alluded to in chapter 2) that awareness plays a key role in has to do with the assignment of blame. Some of you blame others more than is fair. Others of you blame yourselves more than is fair. Nobody has perfect awareness and assigns responsibility accurately all the time. I have heard it said that we are each responsible for 50 percent of our relationship with other people. And it is only when we start to develop better awareness that we can start to take full responsibility for our part and our part only. The book described how we teach other people how to treat us. And the reality is that we (presumably being the non-HC person in the interaction) often contribute to the escalation of the "problem person" outside of our awareness by our responses.

This poses one of the biggest challenges of dealing with difficult people: managing our personal reactivity. We must recognize thoughts we have in response to what others say or do before we can make efforts to change them, which is necessary for responding differently and getting better results in our relationships. So all of this is to say: we can have all the "head knowledge" this book has covered, but if we don't continue to improve our awareness regularly, we cannot use it to deal with the challenging people in our lives, and this knowledge is basically useless.

Application

The iconic founder of rational emotive therapy, Dr. Albert Ellis, once said in a training of his I attended that "a psychotherapy that helps people feel better when they leave the session but does nothing to actually improve their lives is essentially useless." I feel the same way about books and conferences. I have long believed that the person who says "wow, that was amazing" in response to reading one of my books or attending one of my trainings but leaves with no practical takeaways to help themselves, their students, their staff, or their clients has essentially wasted their time and money.

As we develop awareness, we must then use our knowledge to facilitate growth in our interactions with people. Chapter 12 walked you through how to identify and target the difficult people in *your* life. This section will not replicate that. It is not that specific. Rather, it is a bigger picture challenge to you to continue developing your awareness and build your skills in people handling. Once you have identified your tendencies revealed to you by your DISC profile, practice noticing them in yourself regularly.

I am not a huge fan of journaling in general, but occasionally, when done for a specific purpose, it can be a powerful tool. Some people find it helpful to have a time of reflection at the end of every week. Or, even better, every day. If you have strong *D* tendencies, ask yourself questions like: "In my quest for accomplishment was I overbearing to anyone today?" If your primary style is an *I* consider possibilities like "Could my need for recognition have rubbed anyone the wrong way during this project?" If *S* is the style that you have the most of, reflect on questions like "Is it possible that my need to connect with people could have negatively impacted anyone else or hurt the effort of my team in any way today?" Finally, if you have strong **C** traits, ask yourself questions like "Did my need for completeness and detail cause me to fail to complete a required task by the deadline this week?"

See appendix D for a more comprehensive list of awareness-enhancing reflection questions for each style.

For most people, change occurs by initially reflecting on historical events from recent experiences or interactions. Eventually, it becomes possible to develop the ability to notice and respond "in the moment." That is, it is common to first notice in a daily reflection, "Wow, I didn't realize it at the time, but thinking back on it I might have really hurt Melissa's feelings when I urged people to get moving in the meeting." And, after paying attention to your tendencies over time, you will eventually recognize *in* the meeting *as* you give a directive that a person is shutting down that the volume of your voice may have inadvertently turned itself up a few notches and changed how you communicated in that very meeting.

Learn the skills that don't come naturally to people with your personality style that might require some effort to develop. Then look for opportunities to use them. In my coaching programs, this consists of three distinct steps:

1. Awareness—Dealing with blind spots that keep people from seeing their roles in problematic interaction.
2. Skill building—Learning the communication skills they do not possess that are needed.
3. Practical application—Using the skills in the situations and with the people you need to use them in/with.

This underscores a huge gap in the therapy and coaching world. I recently had a client who, after unsuccessfully attempting therapy for five years, spent $8,000 on a coaching program related to self-esteem and assertiveness. I quickly discovered why, in spite of "putting the work in," she did not achieve her desired outcome. She knew the material like the back of her hand, and she could have TAUGHT a high-quality assertiveness class. But she could not *use* the skills with the two people in her life she needed to the most: her boyfriend and her mother.

So successful outcome involves both *learning* a skill and then *using the skill* intentionally in the area of life that it is needed. Being a highly ranked tennis player in the state of Kansas in my high school and then in my small college days, this came intuitively to me. When learning to play tennis, I first received instruction on how to hit the various strokes; and then I perfected them by doing countless drills. I hit thousands of forehands, backhands, volleys, serves, overhead smashes, and so on. But then once I knew *how* to execute the strokes, then I had to learn strategy. This is where the individual coaching came in. I could have the best volleys in the conference, but if I hit them from the baseline, I would probably lose. I could have a killer drop shot, but if I attempted to use them when my opponent was already at the net, I likely would not have much success.

Similarly, when dealing with HC people, having the knowledge of how to handle them is not enough. Skill building and intentional action are key.

So learn these skills. Then look for opportunities to use them. Seek assistance if you need to. I help my clients set up opportunities to develop these. Life also presents us with many "happy accidents" where we are given invitations to practice our skills.

For instance, I personally honed my assertiveness sitting through multiple time-share presentations. I learned to anticipate questions. I learned to respond assertively but not aggressively. I worked on challenging back. I learned the delicate art of polite interruption. If they didn't take my no for an answer I called them out on it. If I had to, I asked them why they continued to disrespect me and advised them that being impolite to potential clients was probably not the best way to get business.

Another practical way to work on assertiveness, if this is a skill that feels unnatural to you, is by taking those dreaded spam telemarking calls most people simply ignore and send to their voicemail. Script out what you will say to them. Have some fun with it! Welcome spam! See those calls as opportunities for growth. Pay attention to the tone of your voice as you talk to them. Observe if and when your emotions escalate. Notice if you are erring on the side of passivity or aggression. Work to dial it up or step it back in small ways in that conversation. Use these calls as a lab to practice your skills! You have nothing to lose!

If your attention to detail serves you well in your job but hurts you in your personal relationships, look for day-to-day opportunities to "tolerate sloppy." When your spouse makes the bed halfway and the comforter has wrinkles from head to toe, resist the urge to criticize. Perhaps even thank them for making it! If people-pleasing has caused you problems and is an area you have identified for growth, look for opportunities to say no. Start small. Say no to solicitors or people at the grocery store that, in theory, you care very little about what they think. Then look for small, even if insignificant ways to say no to your fellow teachers, a member on a board on which you serve, or a church member. Finally, try to use the skills with a parent, a partner, a child or whoever is most important to you. Looking for and even welcoming opportunities for personal development in the specific areas we are challenged can be uncomfortable at first, but well worth it in the long run. And these are the action steps required if we truly want to achieve the complete freedom we desire in our relationships.

Once you have the awareness to recognize situations that might call for certain people handling skills, and you have a set of such skills in your toolbox, now it is time to employ strategy. Being intentional in our interactions starts with, as Stephen Covey put it, beginning with the end in mind. Ask yourself the question, "What do I really want out of this interaction?" before doing or saying anything. We need to have clarity about what your goals of the interaction are. What is your desired outcome? Before we have certainty on this, we can't know how best to proceed in a given situation.

How you proceed may also be influenced by your relationship to the person. Is there a power imbalance? If they are your supervisor, administrator, or authority figure of some kind this will need to inform our approach. Similarly, if *you* are the authority figure, a different set of dynamics is in play that needs to be considered. Are they a family member? A parent? A child? A sibling? A coworker, fellow student, or congregation member? Considering not only the goal of the interaction but the dynamics of the relationship can go a long way toward having an effective encounter.

While far too many nuances in dynamics or interactional possibilities exist to cover exhaustively here (this is where personal coaching comes in), I'd like to highlight one more important principle in terms of tactics while having these challenging conversations. This is the often-misunderstood principle of *choosing your battles*.

First, not every battle is yours to fight. Some people, particularly people with "control issues," want to jump in and intervene every time they see something they don't like. But ask yourself this question: "Is this really my battle to fight?" More bluntly put: "What makes this any of my business?"

Secondly, if we decide this does concern us and is a battle we will choose to fight, we can be strategic about *how* we fight it. Different approaches are more effective in different situations. Remember, sometimes many well-meaning people say things that make their workplace or classroom environments worse. I will never forget the flight I was on (can you tell I have spent a good percentage of my life on planes?) that the pilot came on the PA system and made an announcement in broken and only partially discernible English saying something about "much turbulence between here and Edmonton." A couple of sentences later other passengers and I could make out the phrases "plenty of fuel" and "in case we need to make an emergency landing" to which the lady next to me yelled a sarcastic "thanks for that!"

The lesson I learned, or at least had reinforced that day, was that if we can't communicate something clearly, sometimes it is best to not say anything at all! A related principle in having difficult conversations is that just because something is true doesn't mean it needs to be said. When you have your "end in mind," this can influence when, if, and how you respond. Ask yourself the question, "Even though ABC is true, if I say it will it increase or decrease the likelihood of meeting my goal in this conversation?" Some personality styles will have to resist the urge to "prove them wrong." Others may want to avoid conflict. Many other potential unhelpful motives exist as well. Asking ourselves this question serves to "check ourselves" and ensure what we are about to say or do will really serve the end goal rather than our personality-driven ulterior motives that can so often creep to the surface when we get our buttons pushed and our autopilots take over. Many clients I work with come into coaching or therapy with mindsets that foster internal dialogues, telling them things like, "If I don't say something, it's a sign of weakness." There are many variations of this that differ for everyone. But the person with these thinking traps would do well to internalize the idea that there is a big difference between not speaking up because one *can't* versus not speaking up because one *chooses not to* because it is not in the best interest of that interaction.

The legendary basketball coach and motivational figure John Wooden is famous for saying "Never let the peaks get too high or the valleys get too low." I believe this is sound advice for any of us who are regularly around these types of people who seem to have the unique superpower of influencing the mood of those around them. Because the various types of HC people can be draining to be around and affect our emotional states and behavior in many negative ways if we fail to handle them effectively, the final question I will leave you with is this:

Who are you becoming in the face of your difficult person?

Are you allowing them to rob you of your joy?

Are you becoming that negative cynical dude or that angry chick with the chip on your shoulder nobody wants to be around? Did you once feel a passion or a purpose in your life that has been dowsed in the face of one or more of these people?

Becoming "this person" is often a slippery slope and happens in such small increments. Many people do not realize they have allowed a difficult person (or people) over time to influence them to become someone they never were and frankly oftentimes a person they do not like. Examine yourself. Ask others for input. Remember, due to blind spots, the best way to get an honest appraisal of how we really come across is by asking others we trust who see us more accurately than we see ourselves and are willing to shoot straight with us. If this happens to you, even to a small degree, I want to encourage you to take the steps you need to reclaim your former self. For some people, the mere act of taking a self-focus and investing in personal development work is difficult due to programing that tell us this work is "selfish." If you have some of this mindset in you, keep in mind that investing in yourself is actually investing in the lives of those people you influence and ultimately investing in your ability to fulfill your purpose/calling.

Many of you may be familiar with the parable of the bricklayer, that has had different iterations over the years, but is based on a real-life story that dates to the sixteenth century. The version I have heard goes something like this:

After the great fire of 1666 that leveled London, the world's most famous architect, Christopher Wren, was commissioned to rebuild St. Paul's Cathedral. One day in 1671 Christopher Wren observed three bricklayers on a scaffold, one crouched, one half-standing, and one standing tall, working hard and fast. To the first bricklayer, Christopher Wren asked the question, "What are you doing?" To which the bricklayer replied, "I am a bricklayer, I am laying bricks to feed my family."

The second bricklayer responded, "I am a bricklayer, I am building a wall." The third bricklayer responded, "I am a bricklayer. I am building a great cathedral to the Almighty that will inspire people for years to come."

The third bricklayer's answer reflects Simon Sinek's thinking in asking the now-famous question, *"What's your why?"* Connecting to our purpose can help us cultivate a mindset for more effectively dealing with the difficult people in our life. It can minimize the anger, frustration, anxiety, and other emotional angst these people who drive us nuts seem to have a unique power to elicit in us. Whether your "why" is related to a higher spiritual purpose, living your life consistent with a moral compass or sense of meaning that is important to you, or fulfilling organizational mission, this higher-level thinking can help get our attention out of the "weeds" and focused on the more meaningful, long-term, bigger picture.

Nobody likes to deal with difficult people. But the reality is that we don't get a choice *if* we will encounter them. Our only choice is how we respond *when* we do. Do we allow them to continue to drive us nuts? Or do we learn to handle them strategically, effectively, and with integrity so we can be content with what we see when we look ourselves in the mirror each morning? My hope is this book will help you do the latter.

APPENDIX A

Table of Traits: Greatest Strength or Greatest Weaknesses?

Our greatest strengths, if not contained, can become our greatest weaknesses. This is the essence of personality. Traits that serve us well in one context don't necessarily serve us well in others. This underscores the difference between a "*symptom*" and a "*trait*." A symptom (a fever, swelling, high blood pressure) is never a good thing. But a trait is not inherently "good" or "bad"—it is just more or less helpful depending on its extremity OR its context. Appendix D expands on an idea of flexibility discussed in chapter 2 and briefly illustrates its importance by highlighting how traits in each type of HC individual covered in the book can be helpful as well as unhelpful.

Type of HC Person	Trait Exhibited	How it Could Help	How it Could Hurt
The Bully	Confidence	Decision-making, initiative, positive image	"Acts before thinking" and makes big mistakes
The Bully	Low Empathy	Not held captive by approval of others	Runs over people, damages relationships
The Con Artist	Rule Breaking	Not impeded by "unnecessary" guidelines	Breaks major rules, regulations, or laws

The Con Artist	Low anxiety	Operates in high-risk situations feeling no pressure	No moral compass, perpetrates atrocities
The Drama Mamma	Image conscious	"Presents well," showcases the positive	Style over substance, misses what is important
The Drama Mamma	Attention-seeking	Entertaining, spontaneous, fun to be around	Insensitive to others, consequences of Impulsivity
The Victim	Past-oriented thinking	Doesn't brush important things under the rug	Has difficulty letting go, moving forward
The Victim	"Whistleblower" traits	Exposes true corruption, abuse of power	Exaggerated accusations, frivolous complaints
The Land Mine	Passion	Energizes others	Drains others
The Land Mine	Dichotomous thinking	Loves you	Hates you
The Yes Man (or Ma'am)	Dependency	Never acts rashly/impulsively	Needy, clingy, draining
The Yes Man (or Ma'am)	Approval-seeking	Values options of others	Can't make decisions on own when need to
The Overanalyzer	Critical thinking	Finds errors others miss	Perceived as negative in relationships
The Overanalyzer	Repetitive	Does high-quality work	Misses time deadlines
The Skeptic	Suspiciousness	Sniffs out actual threats	Misreads people's intentions, unapproachable
The Skeptic	Asks many questions	Elicits much information	Annoys others, slows down work efforts

APPENDIX B

Belief Based Validation Statements for Each HC Type

Every conversation is different. Every person is different. Every organization, school, and church is different. Relationships have different dynamics. Objectives in given situations are different. So this appendix is in no way a comprehensive template for you to "fill in the blank this way" and the work is done. Dealing with people is far too complex of an art and science for that. And again the goal here is not to manipulate people. You and God know your heart. But the following appendix is intended to serve as a brief reminder of the mindsets involved in each type of difficult person you may deal with and give you a quick start guide for starting each conversation in a way that speaks their language.

The Bully
⌘ "I know you are extremely busy and your time is valuable, but I was wondering if ..." (make it quick).

The Con Artist
⌘ "It might be pushing the limits just a little bit, but I wondered if we ..."

The Drama Mamma
⌘ "You know what I thought would be super fun and I knew you were the go-to girl for? ..."

The Victim

⌘ "I know this wasn't fair and I can't even imagine the pain—and what would really help us is ..."

The Land Mine

⌘ "I can't imagine what that must have felt like—it sounds like the worst I could ever understand—I want you to know that I am here for you and I would like to ..."

The Yes Man (or Ma'am)

⌘ "Since you may be the person here that values people on the team the most, I thought you would be the person I could count on to help with ..."

The Overanalyzer

⌘ "Since attention to detail is so important for this project, I knew you were the one I could count on to get the job done right. Here's exactly what we need ..."

The Skeptic

⌘ "I can't have someone who naively believes everything they hear in this role. Can I trust you to look out and protect us by doing ...?"

APPENDIX C

Softening Statements– Take Responsibility!

Oftentimes our BAM validation statements work like magic. But sometimes they get misconstrued. Other times, simply due to *our* styes, *we* can rub people the wrong way. When this happens, it is important to take responsibility for our part, recognizing our specific tendencies and then attempting to rebuild rapport so we can move the conversation forward. The following style "softening statements" can help you lead into these conversations:

The D

⌘ "Got it. I know I can be pretty direct sometimes. I promise I did not mean to hurt your feelings. What can I do to help us move forward?"

The I

⌘ "I see what's happening. I have been known to exaggerate from time to time. I'll try not to get distracted from here on. What would you like me to be doing now?"

The S

⌘ "I am so sorry. I know I love to talk and sometimes I overwhelm people. I'll get right to it."

The C

⌘ "I hear you. I have given too many details. I know I have a tendency to get lost in the weeds at times. I'll try to get to the larger point sooner next time."

APPENDIX D

Journaling Reflection Questions for the Four DISC Styles

Because we all have blind spots in our personalities, sometimes our styles drive us to behave in ways that hurt our ability to respond effectively to the difficult people in our lives. And sometimes these autopilot behaviors hurt us in other ways outside our awareness. This appendix offers a few journaling questions to reflect on for each of the four DISC styles that can help us develop insight into how our actions might hurt us in ways we were not aware of and push us to strive for growth in those areas. It is optimal to do these entries daily, but many choose to do so weekly.

The D
In my haste to "accomplish" or "succeed" this week, is it possible I could have run over anyone or hurt someone's feelings in the process?

_____
_____
_____

If so, who?

_____
_____
_____

Who could I ask to check out others' perceptions of my behavior in possibly harmful interactions?

_____

_____

_____

Is there anything about my *D* style that influenced me to violate my personal values this week? If so, how?

_____

_____

_____

_____

Do I owe anyone an apology or would it be in my best interest to make amends? Who/why?

_____

_____

_____

What changes would I like to make this week to use my "driven" traits in more helpful ways?

_____

_____

_____

In what ways did my decisive traits help me this week I want to continue to use my powers for good in the week to come?

_____

_____

_____

Final reflections

_____
_____
_____
_____
_____
_____
_____
_____

The I

In my attempt to be spontaneous and fun, could my joking, flirtatious behavior, or teasing have done harm in any way I didn't notice at the time? If so, how?

_____
_____
_____

Could my need to be the center of attention have hurt any person/team goal outside my awareness?
If so, who/what?

_____
_____
_____

Who could I ask to check out others' perceptions of my behavior in possibly harmful interactions?

_____
_____
_____

Is there anything about my *I* style that influenced me to violate my personal values this week? If so, what behavior(s)? Which value(s)? In what way?

_____

_____

_____

Do I owe anyone an apology or would it be in my best interest to make amends?

_____

_____

_____

What changes would I like to make this week to use my "in" traits in more helpful ways?

_____

_____

_____

In what ways did my spontaneous traits help me this week I want to continue to use my powers for good in the week to come?

_____

_____

_____

Final reflections

_____

_____

_____

_____

_____

_____

The S

Could my need to make sure everyone else was OK have hurt either my or anyone else's ability to accomplish something this week? If so, how?

_____

_____

_____

Could my need to make sure I had others' approval have hurt me in any way this week? If so, how?

_____

_____

_____

Was there any way I could have accidentally enabled someone else's harmful behavior by rescuing them from their consequences this week?

_____

_____

_____

Did my attempts to help people in my life this week really help them? In what ways could it have hurt?
Is there anything about my *S* style that influenced me to violate my personal values this week?

_____

_____

_____

Do I owe anyone an apology or would it be in my best interest to make amends? Who and why?

_____

_____

_____

What changes would I like to make this week to use my spontaneous/fun style in more helpful ways?

_____

_____

_____

In what ways did my social personality help me this week that I want to continue to those powers for good in the week to come?

_____

_____

_____

Final reflections

_____

_____

_____

_____

_____

The C

In my attempt to "get things right," did I miss any deadlines this week?

_____

_____

_____

Did my need to stay intently task-focused hurt any relationships this week? If so which one(s)?

_____

_____

_____

If so, what steps might I need to take to restore them?

_____

_____

_____

Did my tendency to miss the "forest for the trees" cause me to miss any big picture thinking that could have benefitted me this week?

_____

_____

_____

In what other ways could my perfectionistic traits have hurt me this week that I did not notice?

_____

_____

_____

In what ways might I harness those traits to help me this week versus hurt me?

_____

_____

_____

In what ways did my perfectionistic traits help me this week I want to continue to use my powers for good in the week to come?

_____

_____

_____

Final reflections

_____

_____

_____

_____

_____

_____

_____

_____

Bibliography

American Psychiatric Association. *Diagnostic and Statistical Manual of Mental Disorders, 5th Edition: DSM-5.* The American Psychiatric Association, 2013.

Antony, Martin. *When Perfect Isn't Good Enough.* New Harbinger Publications, 2009.

Babiak, P and Hare, Robert D Snakes in Suits: When Psychopaths Go to Work. 2007.

Baker, J. Mission: Mission, Vision, Values and Distinctives are Established and Agreed Upon Sacred Structures, April 9, 2019 https://sacredstructures.org/mission/the-story-of-three-bricklayers-a-parable-about-the-power-of-purpose/.

Beck, AT. *Cognitive Therapy and the Emotional Disorders.* Plume, 1979.

Beck, A.T. *Cognitive Therapy of Personality Disorders.*

Behary, W. *Disarming the Narcissist.* New Harbinger Publications, 2021.

Cloud, H and Townsend, J. (2017*) Boundaries. When to Say Yes, How to Say No to Take Control of Your Life.*

Covey, Stephen, R. *The 7 Habits of Highly Effective People: Powerful Lessons in Personal Change*, 2004. Free Press.

Discovery Report Assessment Validation Study Results (DISC Model of Human Behavior). Calculations Performed by Thomas G. Snider-Lotz Ph. D., Psychometric Statistician.

Eagles, Matthew. *Old English Dictionary.* New Generation Publishing, 2020.

Ellis, A. Personal Communication. Live Training. 1999.

Epictetus, *Discourses*, Book II, ch. 17.

Flemming, V., Cukor, G and Wood, 1939. *Gone with the Wind*. Metro-Goldwyn Mayer (MGM).

Foster, Jody. (2020) *The Schmuck in My Office: How to Deal Effectively with Difficult People at Work*. MacMillan.

Gibbons, Serenity Forbes "You and Your Business Have 7 Seconds to Make a First Impression: Here's How to Succeed" June 2018.

Goldfried, Marvin, R. "Cognitive-Behavior Therapy: Reflections on the Evolution of a Therapeutic Orientation." *Cognitive Therapy and Research*, Vol. 27, No. 1, February 2003.

Haislop, T. "Aaron Hernandez Timeline: From Murders to Trial to Prison Suicide." The Sporting News Online. 1/18/20.

MD Laird, P Harvey, J Lancaster. "Accountability, Entitlement, Tenure, and Satisfaction in Generation Y." *Journal of Managerial Psychology* 30(1), 87–100.

Jung, C. *Psychology of the Unconscious*. Dover Publications, 2003.

Kilner, J.M, R. N. Lemon. What We Know About Mirror Neurons?

Kreger, R and Mason, P. *Stop Walking on Eggshells: Taking Your Life Back When Someone You Care About Has Borderline Personality Disorder*. 2020. New Harbinger Publications.

Leahy, Robert, L (2003). *Overcoming Resistance in Cognitive Therapy*. Guilford.

Leahy, R. Personal Correspondence, 2003.

Lee, Christopher. (2020). Performance Conversations: How to Use Questions to Coach Employees, Improve Performance, and Boost Confidence. Society for Human Resource Management.

Lester, Greg. *Power with People: How to Handle Just About Anyone, to Accomplish Just About Anything*, 2014.

Maxwell, J. *Everyone Communicates, Few Connect.* Thomas Nelson, 2010.

Maslow, Abram. 1966, *The Psychology of Science.*

Oldham, John. *The New Personality Self-Portrait: Why You Think, Work, Love and Act the Way You Do.* Bantam, 1995.

Pettibon, Patrick, D. Why DISC is Easier to Remember Than MBTI. 2017.

Prochaska, James, O. Changing for Good: A Revolutionary Six Stage Program for Overcoming Bad Habits and Moving Your Life Positive. 1994.

Robert Rohm. Personality Insights, "Tip: Being Task Oriented AND People Oriented is a Great Combination! 2019.

Rohm, R. *Positive Personality Profiles: D-I-S-C-over Personality Insights to Understand Yourself and Others!* Voyages Press Inc 2005.

Ramani Durvasula. (YouTube Channel) https://www.youtube.com/c/DoctorRamani?app=desktop.

SHRM Report Foundations Effective Practice Management Guidelines: Retaining Talent.

David G. Allen, SHRM Foundations Effective Practice Guidelines Series. Retaining Talent: A Guide to Analyzing and Managing Employee Turnover. 2008.

Sinek, Simon. *Start with Why: How Great Leaders Inspire Everyone to Take Action.* Portfolio, 2011.

Stout, M. The Sociopath Next Door. 2006. Harmony.

Tolstoy. L. *A Confession*, 1882.

Wargo, E. "How Many Seconds to a First Impression" 2006 APS Observer.

Watzlawick, P et al. (2011). The Principles of Problem Formation and Problem Resolution. Norton.

Ziglar, Z. (2019). *Goals: How to Get the Most Out of Your Life.* Sound Wisdom Publishers.

Take a Deeper Dive!

Take a deeper dive in your personal and professional development by arming yourself with even more strategies to deal with the difficult people in your organization or personal life!

Take the Assessment!

- Take your own personal **disc** assessment and review your profile in a call with Dr. R! Access your assessment at **bit.ly/DrRasmt**
- Take the disk assessment only to learn your precise style blend!
- Assessment PLUS one - time consultation individual consultation

Access the video series! Gain lifetime access to Dr. R's video teaching Series on disarming high conflict Personalities to gain insights not covered in the book that you can refer back to throughout your life when you encounter difficult people. Access video training course at **bit.ly/HCAAP**

Participate in the mastermind! Get your name on the waiting list for the next available slot in a mastermind group! Here you get access to all 12 teaching videos in addition to a weekly mastermind group led by Dr. R himself! Meets Weekly for three months. Access mastermind group at **bit.ly/HCAArP**

Work with Dr. R Individually! Want The full experience? Bring Dr. in to give a Keynote address, provide an in-house training for your organization, or offer targeted coaching/consultation sessions!

Coaching / Consulting packages

- 1:1 Consultation
- In-House Trainings or Keynotes
  For inquiries contact us at difficultpeople@jeffriggenbach.com

Other Publications by Dr. R!

 The CBT Resilience Journal:
21 Days to Develop Immunity
to Adversity in a Pandemic Era

The CBT Coaching and
Counseling Card Deck: 50 Proven
Tools to Promote Personal Growth

 The CBT Toolbox: A Workbook
for Clients, Clinicians, and
Coaches (1st and 2nd editions)

The BPD Toolbox: A Practical,
Evidence Based Guide for
Regulating Emotions

 The Personality
Disorder Toolbox:
The Challenge of the
Hidden Agenda

CPSIA information can be obtained
at www.ICGtesting.com
Printed in the USA
BVHW060837180322
631670BV00008B/694/J